Practical
Suggestions™
for AD/HD

Clare B. Jones

Skill Area: AD/HD
Ages: All ages

LinguiSystems

LinguiSystems, Inc.
3100 4th Avenue
East Moline, IL 61244-9700
1-800-PRO IDEA
1-800-776-4332

FAX: 1-800-577-4555
E-mail: service@linguisystems.com
Web: www.linguisystems.com
TDD: 1-800-933-8331
(for those with hearing impairments)

ISBN 0-7606-0477-0

About the Author

Clare B. Jones, Ph.D., is a nationally-recognized author and presenter in the field of special education. Dr. Jones is the former Director of Education for Phoenix Children's Hospital and Director of Special Education for the Lakewood City Schools. She was also a classroom teacher for over twenty years. Dr. Jones has received numerous awards and honors. She was named Community Educator of the Year by California Resource Specialists, was honored as the Ohio Master Teacher of the Year by the Martha Holden Jennings Foundation, and received the Hall of Fame Award from CHADD (Children and Adults with Attention-Deficit/Hyperactivity Disorder). She is a past President of the Arizona Council for Exceptional Children and the Arizona School Health Association and served as the Chairperson of the State Special Education Advisory Board for three years. Dr. Jones lives in Scottsdale, Arizona, where she maintains a practice, Developmental Learning Associates, L.L.C. She is the author of six books and numerous articles. *Practical Suggestions for AD/HD* is Clare's second publication with LinguiSystems. She is also the author of *The Source for Brain-Based Learning*.

Dedication

This book is dedicated to my daughter, Lindsay Elizabeth Jones. *You have become what I dreamed you could be, and you are on your way to becoming what you dream you will be.*

Cover Design by Mike Paustian
Page Layout by Lisa Parker
Edited by Karen Stontz

Table of Contents

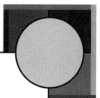

Attention deficit is one of childhood's most frequent disorders, and it is clearly the main reason why most children are referred to mental health clinics today. This disorder, first noted four decades ago, only reached national prominence in the early eighties when it was included in the list of disorders named in the *Diagnostic and Statistical Manual of Mental Disorders-Fourth Edition (DSM-IV)*. It has now gained the respect and research emphasis of both medical and mental health practices. Research has allowed scientists to see the very biological beginnings of this disorder and to predict its course. State-of-the-art detection systems will emerge in the next decade, and families living with attention disorder will see an incredible emphasis on treatment and long-term management. This cutting edge information is welcome to those who live with, educate, or treat individuals with AD/HD* because this disorder creates incredible challenges. To meet the challenges successfully, parents and professionals must stay abreast of the most current information on AD/HD and partner with each other to accomplish the best possible results for the individual with AD/HD. This book is written to provide these two groups of caregivers with the latest research and innovative practices. This text focuses on not what parents and professionals are doing, but rather on what they *must* do.

Each child with an attention disorder is unique, but these children have common characteristics or anomalies that clearly identify them as having the disorder. They are affected by the disorder to different degrees, but the majority falls within the descriptors of the *DSM-IV*. *Practical Suggestions for AD/HD* offers suggestions and strategies to cope with this disorder through the life span. It examines the roles of both the professional and the family. It promotes self-advocacy and self-management, and it offers a time line for caregivers to consult as they seek to "stay ahead" of the syndrome and its path. It will explore the implications of the federal laws serving this population, and it will delve into the new research on the specific differences of the female affected with this disorder. Last, it will serve to exemplify the types of environmental changes, classroom activities, and personal strategies and resources we can use to successfully manage and educate persons with AD/HD.

Clare B. Jones

---

* The term "AD/HD" will be used throughout the book to describe all attention deficit disorders, both inattentive and hyperactive-impulsive.

CLASSIFIEDS

Wanted!

People to join an attention deficit disorder club. Applicants must be inattentive, hyperactive, and impulsive. Call now!

*You may be interested in joining this exciting and diverse club, or you may have someone you would like to recommend for membership! Membership is not exclusive to any race, socio-economic class, or nation. In fact, attention deficit is reported across the board in all societies. Membership is not exclusive to gender; however, the disorder is usually present more often in males than females, at about a four-to-one ratio. The club boasts a membership estimated at four to twelve percent of the entire population. When you join, you receive a lifetime membership. You never need to renew. Once you're in the club, you're **always** in the club!*

202 LOST A

203 EMPLO

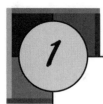
Welcome to the reality of attention deficit hyperactivity disorder! An ad like the one on the previous page seems almost possible today. Parents and professionals dealing with attention deficit disorder are often overwhelmed with the incredible maze of information available on this syndrome. This excess of media and Internet information can lead many to believe that there is actually a club like the one advertised above. This media "over stimulation" evoked a reaction from a woman in my own audience one day who asked, "Dr. Jones, AD/HD is everywhere. Doesn't everyone have attention deficit today?" The answer is **NO, they don't!** Certainly, there are times when we all feel inattentive and distracted. However, people who experience AD/HD encounter it every day in every facet of their lives. They experience difficulties at school, at home, at leisure, and at work. AD/HD is a permanent, not occasional, part of their lives.

This neurobiological disorder was identified in people as early as 1902 and has been mislabeled, over-diagnosed, and misdiagnosed ever since. The fact is Attention Deficit is a disability which is currently the most commonly-diagnosed childhood behavior disorder (Barkley 1998, Pelham et al. 1992). The majority of people with attention disorders are diagnosed when they are in elementary school. The characteristics usually appear well before age seven and endure. In the United States, parents typically seek testing for boys around age eight and for girls around age twelve.

In May of 2000, the American Academy of Pediatrics (AAP) released new recommendations for the assessment of school-age children with AD/HD and stated that approximately 4 to 12% of their patients have the disorder. Males are four times more likely to have the disorder than females (Ross and Ross 1982). The ratio of the population changes at the adult level where statistics report numbers of one adult male to every adult female. The rationale for this change at the adult level is more females who were "missed" at the young adult age are now aware of the disorder and are coming into clinics seeking further information.

The child in your life who regularly wiggles in his chair; who stares dreamily out the window; and whose book bag is an eruption of old papers, banana peels, and trading cards may not be a lazy, unmotivated student but rather a child with attention deficit hyperactivity disorder. The *Diagnostic and Statistical Manual of Mental Disorders-Fourth Edition (DSM-IV)*, published by the American Psychiatric Association, identifies AD/HD as a syndrome that interferes with an individual's ability to focus (inattention), to regulate his activity level (hyperactivity), and to inhibit behavior (impulsivity). These behaviors may seem typical to most young children, but when they persist for at least six months and begin to negatively impact learning and normal living, it becomes critical to examine them in more depth.

> *One father recently told me, "When the middle school teachers met with my wife and me in a parent conference, they showed us all of my son's report cards from kindergarten to present. Through the years, every teacher had made almost identical comments about his behavior, activity, and focus. The teachers showed me that this was a chronic pattern that had not changed."*

Diagnosis for AD/HD should not be made from one specific medical test or observation. Rather, it should be an in-depth look at behaviors, family and medical history, psychological tests, and performance over a period of at least six months, and symptoms must be observed in at least two settings such as home and school.

Identifying the Criteria

To consider the diagnosis, the evaluator must follow specific guidelines. The criteria for diagnosis are found in the *DSM-IV*. Expert physicians and psychologists created the manual to help identify and classify mental health terms and symptoms for the mental health professional. Figure 1-1, page 10, shows the current criteria as designated by the manual in the year 2000.

Figure 1-1: Diagnostic Criteria for Attention Deficit/Hyperactivity Disorder

I. Either A or B

    A. Six (or more) of the following symptoms of **inattention** have persisted for at least six months to a degree that is maladaptive and inconsistent with developmental level:

       1. often fails to give close attention to details and makes careless mistakes in schoolwork, work, or other activities

       2. often has difficulty sustaining attention in tasks or play activities

       3. often does not seem to listen when spoken to directly

       4. often does not follow through on instructions and fails to finish schoolwork, chores, or duties in the workplace (not due to oppositional behavior or failure to understand instructions)

       5. often has difficulty organizing tasks and activities

       6. often avoids, dislikes, or is reluctant to engage in tasks that require sustained mental effort (such as schoolwork or homework)

       7. often loses things necessary for tasks or activities (e.g., toys, pencils, school assignments, books, or tools)

       8. is often easily distracted by extraneous stimuli

       9. is often forgetful in daily activities

    B. Six (or more) of the following symptoms of **hyperactivity-impulsivity** have persisted for at least six months to a degree that is maladaptive and inconsistent with developmental levels:

      Hyperactivity

       1. often fidgets with hands or feet or squirms in seat

       2. often leaves seat in classroom or in other situations in which remaining seated is expected

       3. often runs about or climbs excessively in situations in which it is inappropriate (in adolescents or adults, may be limited to subjective feelings of restlessness)

       4. often has difficulty playing or engaging in leisure activities quietly

       5. is often "on the go" or often acts as if "driven by a motor"

       6. often talks excessively

      Impulsivity

       7. often blurts out answers before questions have been completed

       8. often has difficulty awaiting turn

       9. often interrupts or intrudes on others (e.g., butts into conversations or games)

II. Some hyperactive-impulsive or inattentive symptoms that caused impairment were present before age seven.

III. Some impairment from the symptoms is present in two or more settings (e.g., school [or work] and at home).

IV. There must be clear evidence of clinically significant impairment in social, academic, or occupational functioning.

V. The symptoms do not occur during the course of a Pervasive Developmental Disorder, Schizophrenia, or other Psychotic Disorder and are not better accounted for by another mental disorder (e.g., Mood Disorder, Anxiety Disorder, Dissociative Disorder, or a Personality Disorder).

(American Psychiatric Association 2000)

Subtypes

The diagnosis is divided into four primary subtypes:

1 **Primarily Inattentive Type (AD/HD-IN)**

Many people refer to this as ADD, but the true scientific description is AD/HD inattentive type with the slash (/) indicating with or without hyperactivity.

2 **Primarily Hyperactive-Impulsive Type (AD/HD-HI)**

3 **AD/HD Combined Type (AD/HD-CB)**

The individual meets the criteria for both of the above subtypes.

4 **AD/HD Not Otherwise Specified**

The individual exhibits some characteristics but an insufficient number of symptoms to reach a full diagnosis. These symptoms do disrupt everyday life.

Differences between Inattentive Type (AD/HD-IN) & Hyperactive-Impulsive Type (AD/HD-HI)

Although these two subtypes are very similar, they each have some distinctive features. These features often are apparent from early childhood and are best observed by parents and other caregivers. Inattentive (IN) children tend to be easy, mellow babies while hyperactive-impulsive infants (HI) tend to be extremely active, move frequently, and can be behaviorally disruptive. Classroom teachers report that often the inattentive child has more academic problems whereas the hyperactive child has more behavioral concerns (Solanto 2002).

Inattentive vs. Hyperactive

AD/HD-IN	AD/HD-HI
Problem controlling attention	Problem controlling response
Cannot process quickly	Cannot restrain behavior
Frequent daydreams	Frequent movement
Socially ignored	Socially rejected
Apathetic, unmotivated	Disruptive, hyper
Less aggressive	More aggressive
Space cadet, confused	Antisocial
Lower verbal interaction	Excessive talking
Difficulty paying attention to the main aspects of a task	Difficulty staying with tasks & completing them
Forgetful in daily activities	Weak organization & planning skills
Disorder of posterior brain	Disorder of frontal lobe inhibition

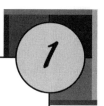

Levels of Severity

> *In my practice I have a family with eleven children. Both parents have been diagnosed with attention disorders, as have six of their children. Of the six children with diagnosed AD/HD, four have the hyperactive components and two have inattentive symptoms. Their symptoms range from mild to moderate to one child with severe complications.*

Attention deficit can be *mild* with few, if any, symptoms in excess of those required to make the diagnosis. The disorder can be *moderate*, which is halfway between mild and severe. Moderate is the category given to the majority of school-age children. The disorder can also be *severe* with additional symptoms beyond what someone needs to make the diagnosis. A parent of a child with attention deficit will want to know and be familiar with the severity of the child's diagnosis to better be able to serve the child over his life span. Figure 1-2 lists the criteria for mild, moderate, and severe levels of attention deficit.

Figure 1-2: Levels of Criteria

Mild   Few, if any, symptoms in excess of those required to meet the diagnosis and no or minimum impairment in school and/or social functioning

Moderate Symptoms of functional impairment ranging between mild and severe

Severe   Many symptoms in excess of those required to make the diagnosis, plus significant and pervasive impairment in function at home, in school, and with peers

(American Psychiatric Association 1987)

Recognizing the Symptoms

AD/HD impedes a person's capacity to sustain attention (predominantly with recurring tasks) and interferes with her ability to manage her emotions and activity level efficiently. It obstructs her capacity to respond constantly to consequences, and perhaps most significantly, to reduce impulsivity. People with AD/HD lack self-regulation and control. This influences their responses in daily living tasks, test taking, and decision making. They appear egocentric and self-serving based on their inattention to others' feelings or needs. Individuals with AD/HD might know what to do, but they are inconsistent in doing what they know because of their inability to stop and think efficiently before responding, regardless of the setting or task (Goldstein 1999). Children who demonstrate inconsistent attention will often appear insensitive to social cues. They will be viewed as self-centered, and they will respond in an immature way, particularly in same age group activities. Their weak memories will affect their recall of important dates, numbers, and facts. Therefore they may appear confused, scattered, or unconcerned when asked to recall information.

The Effects of an Attention Disorder

Lack of attention results in:

- insensitivity to social cues
- appearance of egocentricity
- poorly planned responses to social demands

Weak memory results in:

- difficulty with recall of names, dates, facts, appointments, addresses, and phone numbers
- poor sense of time and time management
- no benefit from normal social experiences

Inefficient sequential skills result in:

- difficulty with social prediction
- problems reading nonverbal feedback

Impulsivity results in:

- careless-appearing responses
- prone to take risks without thinking about the consequences
- random thinking

Long-Term Prognosis

Characteristics of the disorder arise in early childhood, usually before the age of seven. The disorder is considered chronic and persistent through the life span. School-age children with AD/HD are at greatest risk for academic under-achievement, retention, and emotional problems. Some young adults report they experience a reduction of symptoms around the high school to the adult years; however, AD/HD's general course is that it will continue to affect people in different ways as they age. The person who has experienced a reduction of symptoms may have learned to cope with the disorder, or his present environment may be more adaptable to his challenges. Some researchers hypothesize that, for some young adults, this feeling of reduction of symptoms may be an internal regulation of the neurotransmitter dopamine levels in the brain, but further studies are needed in this area.

The path of attention deficit/hyperactivity disorder will affect the person in many ways throughout his life span. The symptoms can make an individual with AD/HD vulnerable to failure in school and in social situations. If these problems go untreated, they intensify and can create significant barriers to meeting life's tests. See Figure 1-3, page 16, for the developmental direction of attention deficit when untreated.

Figure 1-3: Developmental Direction of Untreated Attention Deficit

Infant—feeding and sleeping problems, colic, insatiability, irritability, temperamental dysfunction, high level of ear infections and/or allergies

Toddler—unusual over-activity, crankiness, preschool adjustment problems, extreme insatiability

Elementary—impaired focus, distractibility, impulsivity, inconsistent performance, possible hyperactivity, weak short-term memory, visual-motor integration difficulties, forgetfulness in daily activities

Adolescence—restlessness, inconsistent performance, impaired focus, memory problems, gaps in learning cumulative information, maturation difficulties, frustration, daydreaming

 Young Adulthood—vulnerability to underemployment, high level of auto accidents, substance abuse, difficulty with relationships, high level of sexually promiscuous behavior

Later Adulthood—concentration problems, impulsivity, poor self control, frequent interruptions, restlessness, impatience, poor response to stress, irritability, frequent movement, difficulty with relationships

(Jones, C. 1998, Levine, M. 1987, and Teeter, P. A. 1998)

Master of the Odds

As they grow older, some young adults with AD/HD experience further difficulties such as depression or anxiety. Researchers feel that inattention symptoms tend to be the factors that persist more commonly into adulthood. The hyperactive and impulsivity symptoms reportedly diminish in severity with age. Ultimately, a great many of the people with AD/HD learn to adjust. Early identification and treatment can impact the prognosis. Children who were diagnosed early in their primary years, who have had support from their families, and who develop strong social relationships seem to fare better. Successful people with the disorder have learned to come to terms with it and have learned ways to get over or around its hurdles. Their awareness and understanding of the disorder allows them to seek services and develop new habits. They typically create and use strategies to help themselves manage the symptoms. They have frequently worked closely with their physicians, using a therapeutic medication intervention. They become resilient as a result and learn what will support them through the disability. They take charge and are in control of their lives. They are able to learn coping skills, which become their survival skills.

Some people may refer to these "survivors" as Masters of the Odds—people who overcome the risk of attention concerns. I find they often have a cluster of supportive tools which they have embraced and continue to use throughout their life span. On the next page is a list of tools that successful people with AD/HD have used to beat the odds.

Tools of the Trade for Masters of the Odds

- Embrace strategies as a way of handling a problem

- Know they need tools and resources

- Use medication as a tool, not an answer

- Understand that attention deficit is a problem that needs to be thought about and acted upon

- Develop a support network among tutors, family, friends, and coaches

- Use humor to give themselves relief from difficult situations

- Develop an ability/skill/talent where they get positive feedback

- Believe they can succeed and know what they value

More and more people who have AD/HD are beginning to talk openly about their experiences. This is particularly helpful for young people with the disorder as it provides them with role models. The list on the next page identifies some remarkable people with attention disorders who have "made it."

AD/HD HEROES

Jay Leno (comedian)
Anthony Hopkins (actor)
Mariette Hartley (actress)
Fannie Flagg (author & actress)
Mark Wills (country singer)
Rick Fox (professional basketball player)
Payne Stewart (professional golfer, deceased)
Terry Bradshaw (professional football player)
Keith Brantly (Olympic marathoner)
Gary Hall, Jr. (Olympic swimmer)
Bev Isak (Olympic skeleton team member)
Michael Wolff (jazz musician)
Barry Switzer (College Football Hall of Fame
member & former Dallas Cowboys coach)
Gabe Kapler (professional baseball player)

Did they have AD/HD?
Albert Einstein
Michelangelo
Ben Franklin
Ansel Adams

And perhaps your child? Your student?

Cause

It is now apparent that AD/HD is prevalent in family history. Over 70% of the children diagnosed have a parent with the disorder (Biederman et al. 1995). Adopted children appear to have a high probability for the disorder, leading researchers to hypothesize that gene patterns are factors in a proportion of children diagnosed. Studies at the National Institute of Mental Health (NIMH) involving identical twins found that there is a 99% likelihood that both twins will have the disorder. The chances that fraternal twins will both have the disorder are 50%. Family studies suggest that the condition is linked to genetic predisposition, and researchers speculate that 60% of the cases with attention disorders are hereditary. This research suggests that genetics could be considered a risk factor.

New Research Studies

The strong possibility of hereditary dominance has lead researchers to begin to examine possible differences in chromosome patterning. Gene mapping and state of the art chromosome testing have noted a unique disparity in the chromosome pattern of attention deficit children. This current investigation suggests that the D4 gene is defective in the inattentive profile (AD/HD-IN) while the DRD2 gene is defective in the active, impulsive type (AD/HD-HI). Once these new genetic mapping tests become more available, we will be able to use early detection systems. This information will increase efforts of early intervention. There is no doubt in my mind that a specific gene test which can be used to biologically make the diagnosis will be available to physicians within the next decade.

Further investigation using brain imaging instruments suggests that *dopamine*, a neurotransmitter or messenger molecule, appears to be developmentally active and in higher concentration in the brains of individuals with attention deficit.

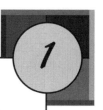

Environmental influences, such as drugs and nicotine, may adversely affect dopamine-rich areas of the brain. Research indicates that if a mother-to-be smoked more than two packs of cigarettes a day, she created a risk factor that significantly influenced the possibility of attention disorders in her unborn child. These assumptions derive from observations that AD/HD is more common in children who had prenatal exposure to drugs or alcohol. A very small percentage of children for whom the diagnosis has been made (roughly less than 1.5%) have the history of exposure to high quantities of lead in the womb and/or an injury to the frontal lobe during the neonatal period.

Smaller Right Brain Section

Researchers studying the formation and shape of the brain note that there appears to be a smaller right front part of the brain in the brains of people diagnosed with AD/HD. Dr. Judith Rapoport, Chief of the Child Psychiatry Branch at the National Institute of Mental Health in Bethesda, Maryland, suggests that smaller parts of the anterior frontal lobe and basal ganglia are present in children with attention disorders. In their quest to determine why this may occur, scientists have also postulated that people with attention deficit do not metabolize or burn sugar fast enough on the right side of the brain.

Ongoing research continues to affirm the impact of genetics, metabolic studies, and smaller right hemisphere structure. The severity of the problems experienced by individuals with AD/HD seems to vary based on life experiences; however, genetics appears to be the primary underlying factor contributing to whether a person will show the symptoms. This cutting edge information is the primary reason why, when redrafting the laws for all handicapped children in 2000, the category "attention deficit" was moved from a mental health description to the specific medical category OHI (Other Health Impaired).

Seeking an Evaluation

If a parent or professional suspects a child may be at risk for attention deficit, the next step is to seek a thorough evaluation for the child. The evaluation is typically the responsibility of a trained mental health professional who has expertise in attention disorders. In a public statement on May 1, 2000, The American Academy of Pediatrics (AAP) recommended that AD/HD evaluations should be initiated by the primary care clinician and should include information from parents or caregivers, as well as school professionals. AAP also recommended that the evaluation should include referrals for further assessment for co-existing conditions. An evaluation for attention deficit disorder would include observation of behaviors and the recording of those behaviors using checklists in everyday settings.

"When the doctor confirmed to me what I really knew in my heart, that Brooke was attention deficit, it was almost a relief. Now I feel like I can take action and do something." —Mother of an AD/HD female

The diagnosis of AD/HD is an all-inclusive process. To ascertain the diagnosis of AD/HD, professionals must conduct a careful evaluation to eliminate other possible causes and determine the presence or absence of co-occurring conditions.

Who Can Make the Diagnosis?

- A physician or primary care physician

- A diagnostic specialist with expertise and skill in attention disorders

- A clinical psychologist, a neuropsychologist, a child or adult psychiatrist with expertise in the area, or a school psychologist

Who Cannot Make the Diagnosis?

- Your neighbor

- The cashier at the grocery store

- A coach

- A talk show host

- Your child's baby-sitter

- A casual observer

How Can a Parent Select the Evaluator?

Parents can choose to use the school-based evaluation team or consult their family physician. Typically, when most parents seek to find someone to give them advice about their children, they will start with the family pediatrician or physician. In some instances, the school district may provide a list of qualified professionals in the area. Once the parent has shared information with the selected professional, they may or may not ask for further testing from the school district.

Parents who suspect their child may have this difficulty will need guidance in where to go first and what steps they need to follow. The following guidelines will help parents know what to ask for when pursuing an evaluation.

Pursuing an Evaluation

• Parents should look for people with expertise in attention disorders. For referrals, go to your local physician or local CHADD (national support group for children and adults with attention disorders) coordinator.

• The evaluator should give checklists to parents, teachers, and any other people who see the child on a regular basis.

• The interview should involve questions concerning the child's health history, school involvement, and developmental milestones.

• The interview or written forms should ask questions about family history.

• The evaluator should spend measurable time interviewing, observing, or testing the candidate.

• If a child is of school age, the evaluator should request information from the school, have teachers submit completed forms, and request handwriting and work samples.

• If necessary, the evaluator should ask for the parents' permission to talk with others involved with the child.

• The evaluator should refer to the *Diagnostic and Statistical Manual of Mental Disorders-Fourth Edition-TR* (2000).

• When the evaluation has been completed, the parent should receive a written report of the information.

How Will the Evaluator Start?

To determine the presence of the symptoms of attention deficit, the evaluator must first gather historical information from parents and teachers. This is usually done in an interview or by having families and educators complete survey-like checklists. In completing the history and other information for the evaluator, the family will be asked to supply family medical records since the evaluator is looking for significant health issues in the past. For example, over 65% of the children diagnosed with attention disorders have a history of ear infections. They also have a higher level of reported allergies and asthma. Recent studies in Israel linked the frequent ear infections and allergies experienced by most AD/HD children to possible deficits in their immune systems. Researchers are not sure why we see this high correlation with these physical symptoms, but it is provocative and further research must be done in this area. The evaluator is also looking for possible head injuries or exposure to drugs, alcohol, or lead toxins during the prenatal period or at birth.

The next step is to request behavioral rating scales completed by both parents and teachers. There are over 45 separate checklists available for the evaluator to consider. They all attempt to get a brief profile of behaviors, impulsivity, and inattention. Below are some selected checklists. These checklists have been typically normed on children with AD/HD and offer comparisons to those not affected with AD/HD.

Selected Checklists

✓ Conners' Rating Scales (long and short versions)

✓ The Achenbach Child Behavior Checklist (CBCL)

✓ The BASC (Behavior Assessment System for Children)

✓ The ANSER System (Aggregate Neurobehavioral Student Health and Educational Review)

✓ The ACTeRS (ADD-H Comprehensive Teachers and Parent Rating Scale)

Note: Addresses and further information regarding these checklists can be found in the Tests & Checklists Cited, pages 204-205.

The checklists help the evaluator comply with the standards for the diagnosis. The DSM-IV states that the diagnosis cannot be made without information from two separate situations (i.e., home and school). The purpose of the checklists is to give the evaluator an interpretation of the child's behavior in two separate environments.

The evaluator may also ask the child to complete a "self-report." Typically, this is introduced to children around age ten. It involves their direct observations or comments about their learning strengths and needs. It is also helpful to have an on-site observation of the child, either at home, at school, or in a play situation in the office or on the playground. The last step should involve a psychoeducational battery, which will offer individual information on personal strengths and weaknesses. Today the most typically used batteries offer subtests that can be influenced by attention, focus, and impulsivity. These tests can confirm the anecdotal research mentioned above, and they also offer a way to specifically see how the disorder is affecting a child's achievement and individual skills. When evaluators have specific information regarding skills, they are better able to design individual accommodation plans based on need.

Key Factors in an Evaluation

⌐⊙ Medical History

⌐⊙ Family History

⌐⊙ Educational History

⌐⊙ Observation—Physical and Interactive

⌐⊙ Parent/Teacher Report Scales

⌐⊙ Social Behavior and Self-Care Skills

⌐⊙ Standardized Testing
(cognitive, basic language skills, motor, sensory, and academic skills)

Standardized Tests

In the area of standardized testing, it is helpful to offer a complete psycho-educational battery to determine specific needs for the student and to evaluate her unique capabilities. The purpose of standardized tests is to gather information about the child's achieved strengths and determine weaknesses, which may affect task production. The test evaluations shown in Figure 2-1 are known to be helpful as part of the process in the diagnosis of attention deficit.

Figure 2-1: Psychoeducational Battery

- *Wechsler Intelligence Scale for Children, Third Edition (WISC-III)*

  Lower scale scores on the following cluster of Wechsler subtests may indicate AD/HD: Arithmetic, Coding, Information, and Digit Span. This grouping of subtests is often referred to as the ACID test. Lower scale scores are those typically below 8.

- *Woodcock-Johnson III (WJ III) Tests of Cognitive Abilities*

  On the Woodcock-Johnson Cognitive, low scores on the following cluster of subtests may indicate AD/HD: #5 Concept Formation, #7 Numbers Reversed, #9 Auditory Working Memory, #14 Auditory Attention, #19 Planning, and #20 Pair Cancellation.

- *Woodcock-Johnson III (WJ III) Tests of Achievement*

- *Wechsler Individual Achievement Test*

- *The Listening Test*

- *The Beery-Buktenica Developmental Test of Visual-Motor Integration (VMI)*

- *Language screening or testing*

Continuous Performance Tests (CPTs)

These computer-generated tests attempt to determine patterns of performance and may be helpful in monitoring medication levels. They are not useful in making the diagnosis alone, but they can be used to generate other information about the student's strengths and weaknesses. Because of their computer game-like format, many children who are skilled game players with experience on game systems like Nintendo and Game Boy may skew the results based on their game competency and not their actual challenge with the disorder.

A recent study by the University of California, San Diego School of Medicine (Schatz et al. 2001) found a risk of over-diagnosis using the TOVA (Test of Variables of Attention), a continuous processing test, noting that it found attention problems in 30% of the control children. Barkley (1991) cautions that the validity of most of the CPTs was low to moderate with some proving unsatisfactory. Computerized tests are not recommended practice at this time.

Guidelines for Professionals When Administering Tests

Experienced test takers know and recognize that a child who is impulsive and hyperactive in a testing situation can affect scores. The following guidelines will help professionals recognize some of the factors that influence the test performance of a child with attention disorders.

Inconsistent Performance
A skilled evaluator will need to be alert to the many behavioral factors that come into play during an evaluation. Children and adults suspected of attention difficulties often display scattered or diffuse scores rather than consistent test performance.

Presentation
Presentation should be noted as a significant part of the evaluation. Observe the child's characteristics and behavior as a part of the testing. Record your observations alongside the scoring.

Impulsivity
The child will often impulsively complete sections of the test with little regard for the directions or sequence. She may not listen to the spoken directions and respond in a haphazard manner.

These responses on testing often reduce the accuracy of the standardized test and may limit the student's total performance. The reliability of the contributing factors must be taken into consideration when reviewing the final scores. The student's true potential may be impaired by these responses. The evaluator will need to comment on the final written report about the observed behaviors. If the evaluator feels they negatively impacted the test results, he should make a statement to that effect.

Additional Factors to Look for in Evaluations

There are specific behaviors that appear to be typical in the performance of children suspected of attention problems. These behaviors are as follows.

1 They appear impulsive on tests of vigilance, completing tasks without planning. If a section of a test involves completing or following sequential directions, they may need the information repeated or they will work ahead without noting the specific information.

2 When asked to write, they will typically print and avoid the use of cursive writing, or they may use a combination of both printing and cursive.

3 In written language exercises, they will frequently leave out capitals, punctuation, and contractions.

4 On specific spelling tests, such as those on *The Woodcock-Johnson III Tests of Achievement*, their error pattern almost appears careless as they leave out letters or add letters. This pattern has been described as an

"eclipsed spelling pattern" (N. Jordan 1987). Errors occur such as *gril* for *girl* and *afrid* for *afraid*. Therefore, you can read their spelling words because they are not incomprehensible, but the error is evident.

5 On classroom spelling tests, teachers will often report to the evaluator that the student knows the words the day of the test, but will have forgotten them by the next day. *Is this why Taylor had to move to new class?*

6 Evaluators will note that suspected AD/HD children often demonstrate excellent memory for the unusual or unique information in their experiences but cannot recall rote or routine information as readily.

7 On short-term memory tasks such as the "Digit Span Test" on the *WISC III* and "Numbers Reversed" on the *Woodcock Cognitive*, evaluators will note an inadequate recall of the verbal number patterns.

8 They tend to do less well on sequential tasks and are more successful on simultaneous tasks (i.e., those tasks that require concurrent thinking).

Emotional Profile

Evaluators will note that the student's emotional profile is described often as "at risk" and noted as highly problematic in the checklists completed by parents and teachers. Their hyperactive and impulsive behavior often interferes with their social learning or emotional maturation. Children suspected as having AD/HD features often demonstrate greater emotional response in their reactions to a task or activity. They are less mature in the self-regulation of emotion because of their deficiencies in behavioral inhibition. Evaluators will note more overt gestures and reactions such as face-making and verbal comments such as, "We have to do what? Oh No! Boring, boring, boring! Get me out of here!"

Making Decisions

The evaluator may also observe that the student will have more difficulty making a decision or choice. The student will either quickly choose an object without careful consideration or will take an inordinate amount of time to decide on a request. She may actually forget the original request as she debates it! She may also be observed impulsively scanning the test materials.

High Stimulus Disorder

As they work, students with attention concerns often are fingering the timer, pencils, papers, etc. Evaluators should note that these students frequently manipulate the materials they are being tested on (e.g., reaching over and turning the page on the test manual for the evaluator). They may get up and wander around the work area and ask for frequent bathroom breaks. Evaluators want to record all of these and other responses that identify any atypical behaviors in their movement, communication skills, and socialization skills. These observations are critical in gathering a true profile of the student but also are important in recording other conditions that may occur. (Note: As many as one-third of children diagnosed with AD/HD also have a co-existing condition.)

Visual Motor Integration

Typically, AD/HD students score about one to two years delayed on tests of visual-motor memory. Careful examination of the tests by the evaluator will indicate the students' errors were of planning and execution, not of visual distortion. On *The Beery-Buktenica Developmental Test of Visual-Motor Integration (VMI)*, a test that requires copying a basic shape, their performance may appear hurried or unfinished. They generally will not display difficulties with configuration or reversal of the drawing, rather they will neglect to count all the lines or dots, will leave out critical lines, and will produce work that resembles a hurried attempt.

Writing Samples

Over half of the children diagnosed with attention disorders exhibit some difficulty with writing, copying from the board, spelling, and letter formation. The evaluator will want to gather handwriting samples to determine and observe the student's written performance. I have found these samples to be a critical part of the evaluation process. If the child is diagnosed with attention disorders and the parents and physician select medication as a therapeutic intervention, then the obtained writing sample becomes a "pretest" document. Following the medication trial, I ask the student to complete a duplicate writing sample and I compare the efforts. In the majority of the cases where medication has been successful, a marked difference is noted in the writing sample. The following positive changes may be observed:

- a positive difference in the spelling pattern
- a reduction in the amount of time it takes the student to write the task
- observed differences in the formation and fluidity of letters
- improvement in legibility

Diagnosis

The evaluation for AD/HD should include a history of family, childhood, academic, behavioral, and social situations. The evaluation process needs to involve the parents, the child, the physician, educational professionals, diagnosticians, and other concerned individuals who work with or know the child. The use of observation, standardized questionnaires, professional guidelines, and related diagnostic tools is necessary.

> *It is well recognized that the best management of AD/HD syndrome requires a multiple–modality approach combining psychosocial and medical interventions.*
>
> —Utah Public Mental Health System, 2002

When the comprehensive evaluation process determines the diagnosis of attention deficit, the first step for parents is to become well informed about the disorder and how it affects their child. From this initial pursuit of objective information, they can begin to consider what treatment, accommodations, or other interventions might be appropriate and desirable for their child. Unfortunately, there is no magic answer to the treatment plan for children with attention deficits. One of the biggest hurdles faced by the practitioner, parents, and individuals with AD/HD is simply the fact that there is no single right solution. It is true that our knowledge about the disorder and how to treat it is changing dramatically, but attention deficit disorder remains a multi-faceted challenge to everyone (C. Jones 1998). The most effective form of management requires a coordinated effort between families, schools, and health professionals. This combined set of plans is called a "multi-modality" intervention.

What Works?

The American Academy of Child and Adolescent Psychiatry (AACAP) stated in their guidelines (1991) "the cornerstones of treatment are support and education of parents, appropriate school placement, and pharmacology." The treatment plan is unique to each individual, yet it will have several core components. Children and adults who manage this disorder have benefited at some time in their lives from the multi-modality tactics shown in Figure 3-1, page 36. These tactics are explained in more detail on pages 37-38.

3

Figure 3-1: What Works?

a) Family understanding of the disorder (parent training, counseling, and support)

b) Behavior therapy and interventions (consistent behavior intervention based on positive reinforcement and mixing in group and individual rewards; the use of "response cost," that is, positive reinforcement combined with punishment)

c) A healthy sense of self-esteem (experiences of success in which peer and family response to the child is positive and immediate; finding an area of success, possibly outside of academic achievement)

d) Medical interventions (drug therapy as a short-term treatment; medication may be just one component in treatment plan)

e) Educational interventions (appropriate educational accommodations provided by knowledgeable teachers and multidisciplinary teams)

f) Counseling (training in social skills, coping skills; and new goal-directed strategies)

(Jones, C. 1998)

---

a) Family understanding is paramount because often other family members have some of the same difficulties. The chances are real that either one or the other parent has similar symptoms. Because of this biological imbalance, children with AD/HD will have specific weaknesses in self-control, attention, and the ability to respond to directions. Families with children with attention disorders will need to approach the treatment plan with a united front (both parents enforcing the same treatment) and with unswerving behavior management. Family members need to understand that attention concerns are considered as much of a disability as wearing glasses, using a hearing aid, or using a wheelchair. They may appear "invisible" when compared to these other more obvious impairments, but they are just as challenging.

b) Behavior interventions and positive reinforcement are another part of the treatment plan. Children with attention difficulties respond to consistency and need structured behavior modification programs. They will appear, at times, to challenge the rules and regulations and will need a variety of techniques to help them succeed. Positive reinforcement coupled with firm, but flexible support will be necessary. Families will want to help the child recognize his strengths and abilities. They need to reinforce successful approaches with praises and reward. One winning technique is to redirect the child when he appears distracted to more productive behavior. Overall, parents will want to encourage self-responsibility and the joy of completing tasks.

c) Self-esteem is commonly defined as the belief that a person is accepted, connected, unique, powerful, and capable (Lavoie 2002). The child with AD/HD often experiences lower self-esteem based on his perception and the perceptions of those around him that he is not as capable as other students. Families and caregivers will want to offer positive rewards for effort, performance, and appropriate choices. This reinforcement will encourage the AD/HD child to feel accepted and successful. Experiences and activities which foster the building of academic and social skills will be helpful. Children should be valued for their personal uniqueness.

d) Medications, particularly psychostimulants, improve attention and social interaction, and sometimes decrease aggression. The majority of children diagnosed with attention concerns benefit from medication. At least 70% to 80% of the children and adults respond positively to psychostimulants. Medication is not used to control behavior but rather to improve the symptoms of the disorder.

e) Educational interventions are a part of the child's success plan. The school environment is a big part of the child's day. It is important that the school environment be supportive of the AD/HD child.   Changes in the school environment may significantly help children with AD/HD. Educational approaches can encourage organization skills, self-planning, developing successful peer relationships, and academic tasks. It is helpful to modify or accommodate the environment to the child's unique needs.

f) Counseling or cognitive-behavioral group therapy provides an opportunity for the child to develop more successful social behaviors and self-control. The child interacts with other peers under the guidance of a therapist. Although research has not shown personal therapy to provide clinically important changes in attention or behavior, it may be helpful in treating symptoms of co-occurring disorders, such as oppositional defiant disorder, depression, or anxiety disorder.

Following is an illustration of the typical steps to the diagnosis, treatment, and life plan of the AD/HD child. This pathway is provided as an overview for parents to follow as they seek support for their child.

Path to . . .

Parent notes child's conflict with attention and focus

School observes child's conflict with attention and focus

Parent brings concerns to physician

Physician guides family to seek further evaluation through private practice specialists or school psychologist

Family history is gathered

Teachers and caregivers complete checklists

Diagnosis is made

Treatment plan is designed

Child is involved

Strategies become life plan

. . . *Success!*

What Doesn't Work?

AD/HD affects a significant population of people; therefore, it creates a magnitude of scientific, public, and media interest. Caring, concerned parents are sometimes swept away with some of the proposed treatment plans which state that they offer an easy remedy. Many of these so called "miracle" treatment plans have not been subjected to rigorous research or trial and yet they make their way into the media, leading some people to believe that they have proven to be successful. Local parent support groups, consumer alert and watchdog groups, and national organizations like CHADD (Children and Adults with Attention-Deficit/ Hyperactivity Disorder) attempt to offer the public timely information on controversial treatment plans. Figure 3-2 lists controversial treatments which, in the opinion of researchers and advocate groups, are not part of the recommended multi-modality treatment plan for attention disorders.

Figure 3-2: Controversial Treatments

- Elimination of sugar or red food coloring from the diet

- Use of anti-motion sickness pills

- High doses of megavitamins and mineral supplements

- Use of Ginkgo (herbal substance)

- EEG biofeedback—Recent studies found that children with AD/HD do not constitute a homogenous group in EEG profile terms

(Clarke, A. R., et al. 2001)

Key Points to Remember about AD/HD

⌐⊙ AD/HD is a neurobiological disorder. Research now indicates that the disorder is biological with a genetic-based profile.

⌐⊙ Parents do not cause AD/HD. Poor parenting, divorce, or parental inconsistency does not cause AD/HD. There are definite skills you can learn to help parent a child with AD/HD, but the diagnosis of AD/HD is biological and present from birth.

⌐⊙ There are varying degrees of attention concerns. Attention Deficit can be inattentive, hyperactive, or a combination of both. It can be mild, moderate, or severe in its symptoms.

⌐⊙ There is no quick fix. The treatment plan for attention disorders is a multi-modality approach. Children and adolescents respond best to multiple approaches to succeed with this disorder.

> *"Good family life is never an accident but always an achievement by those who share it."*
>
> —James H. S. Bossard, 1992

Every day in every city in the United States, parents consult with a doctor or psychologist and leave the office with the diagnosis of Attention Deficit Hyperactivity Disorder for their child. The diagnosis isn't completely unexpected; the parents probably suspected *something* was different about their child since preschool. Even as they gathered the school information for the initial appointment with the doctor, they could see a trend in the completion of the forms and in their own personal comments. No, this is not a surprise. The chances are they even feel somewhat relieved, because now they know what they're dealing with. They recognize they are on the way to identifying how they can help their child be more successful in life. But, what do they do next?

Parent Power

Figure 4-1, page 44, lists some important guidelines for parents just starting to understand their role as the parent of a child with attention disorders. These guidelines are explained in more detail on pages 45-47.

Figure 4-1: Important Guidelines for Parents

a) *Read!*
Read available information. Limit your reading to two or three sources. Choose one book for parents, one for educators, and one general book on the disability.

b) *Network!*
Contact CHADD (Children and Adults with Attention-Deficit/ Hyperactivity Disorder) on the web site at *<www.Chadd.org>* and read their updates and current information. Seek professional assistance and advice.

c) *Set goals!*
Determine a plan for your child and goals for the family.

d) *Inform!*
Notify critical people in your child's life.

e) *Update your skills!*
Brush up on your parenting techniques with the new information you have read.

f) *Tell the child!*
Share the information with the child in a positive, helpful manner.

g) *Gather resources!*
Collect some age-appropriate books and/or magazines for your child to read about the disorder. Locate local services.

h) *Be involved!*
Communicate to and work with the school and individual teachers. An informed parent is an advocate for her child's success.

i) *Be positive and be proactive!*
Know that you can make a difference for your child.

a) Take the resource list the evaluator may have offered you or use the one in the back of this book and head to the library or bookstore. Select a few books or articles to learn about the current information regarding attention deficit. CAUTION! There is so much available that you are bound to be overwhelmed when you begin to seek out the information. Try to select a few books that seem immediately appealing to you and look for the specific issues you are addressing.

b) Locate the CHADD web site at *<www.chadd.org>*, or call them at 1-800-233-4050. CHADD stands for Children and Adults with Attention-Deficit/Hyperactivity Disorder and is a national support organization. Their membership includes periodic updates, newsletters, and an excellent magazine called *ATTENTION!* Place yourself on their web site update list and you will receive continual information throughout the year. You will want to see if there is a CHADD chapter near you. The chapter meetings provide current speakers and up-to-date information along with an opportunity to speak to other parents who have a child with attention concerns.

c) Determine an intervention plan and goal for your child. Read the laws that pertain to children with attention concerns and update yourself on what your child may be eligible for within the school environment. Set up goals and deadlines for steps you want to accomplish. For example, if you decide you want to try to use medication as part of the treatment plan, make an appointment with your physician. Set up a calendar noting the first day medication starts; when the medication will need to be renewed; and any changes in your child's weight, diet, or sleep patterns.

d) Determine which key players in your child's life you will want to inform. This would include your parents, other relatives, teachers, family physician, and other important caregivers in the child's life. If you received a written report from the psychologist or diagnostic specialist making the diagnosis, you will want to

determine whom you will want to read the report and whom you will not. Remember, you are protecting information about your child's disability. You have the right to present it only to those you deem necessary.

e) Review your own behavior techniques and "habits." And, after reading the information about parenting an AD/HD child, employ consistent parenting techniques that are successful with active, inattentive children. You may need to look within in your community for a parenting class or parenting workshop to enhance your present skills. Good resources for these types of classes include your local school district, a local junior or community college, the information desk at your local Chamber of Commerce office, and community recreation departments.

f) Tell your child what the doctor found and what your plan is. Be positive and start by first telling the child about her strengths and strong points. Then briefly review what you have learned, and tell the child there are positive ways to help her limitations with attention and focus. Use one of the many books now written for children of all ages to complete the understanding. An updated list of available books is available through the A.D.D. Warehouse. Order their catalog at 1-800-ADD-WARE.

g) Purchase a large notebook and begin to keep information on attention concerns in it along with your child's report and any information from the school. Use the notebook as a resource tool and an organized way to keep important papers about your child's education handy.

h) Find out what your child's strengths and weaknesses are from the evaluator so you are best prepared to continually guide your child. Typical strong points and noted disadvantages for the attention deficit population are listed on the next page.

Assets	Limitations
verbal expression skills	listening skills
quick application of ideas	follow through of ideas
visual gestalt (big picture thinking) skills	visual recall
long-term memory	short-term memory
intense emotions	impulsivity
generalization of ideas	written language

i) Be patient, positive, and supportive. Recognize that you are working toward the long-term goal of your child being able to cope and succeed with the attention disorder. Be willing to change if something is not working in your plan. Some researchers have noted that the parents of hyperactive children may be overly controlling or overly intrusive (Carlson et al. 1993). Parents may respond

> *One parent told me, "My AD/HD child makes me react like a two year old!"*

more aggressively when parenting this child and develop more tendencies toward negative response to the behaviors. Not understanding the disorder may lead some parents to become more impatient and punitive toward the child. Researchers also have found that parents of AD/HD children experience more feelings of depression and doubt about their own parenting abilities. Parents of AD/HD children are three times as likely to separate or divorce as parents who do not have AD/HD children (Barkley 1994). It is interesting to note that in the research there was reduction in parental negativity and overbearing behaviors when children were treated with medication. Medication works most effectively when it is in conjunction with stable parental support at home (Flint 2001).

A Time Line for the Family

Many families will want a big picture view of what their roles might be over the predicted course of the disorder. Professionals offer the following time line as a vision of the responsibilities and needs at different age ranges. Parents should follow the recommended courses of action.

An Attention Deficit Disorder Time Line for the Family

At the Point of Diagnosis:

- Understand the disorder. Learn what it is and what it is not.

- Introduce bibliotherapy to your child. A selection of books is available for children on the subject of attention disorders. Select several of these books and begin to help your child understand her challenges through stories that describe how other children have succeeded.

- Attend parenting classes and participate in support groups.

- Obtain resources. Information is available at local libraries, in bookstores, on the Internet, and through support groups.

Lower Elementary Grades (first through third grade):

- Inform and involve the teacher. Guide the teacher to understand your child's needs and strengths.

- Encourage your child's personal growth through the selection of outside school activities.

- Confer with a physician on the pros and cons of the use of medication.

- If medication is selected, inform the school and monitor its daily use.

Upper Elementary Grades (fourth through sixth grade):

- This is a critical time to be sure your child is taught study skills and personal organization skills.

- Introduce tactics for school success. Teach self-advocacy and know how your child learns best.

- Support and guide your child in social skills. Help your child adapt to peer groups and to develop team skills and appropriate socialization skills.

Middle School:

- Reinforce and gradually encourage independent skills.

- Teach responsibility.

- Develop a 504 plan if needed. Your child should be involved with the team in plan making. (See Chapter 8, pages 124-125 for a description of this plan.)

- Help your child find or join a group or activity that will provide a social link to other students yet offer the discipline, order, and responsibility your child needs. Suggestions include band, chess club, photography club, drama club, or computer club.

High School:

- Work with a counselor to select teachers and classes that match your child's academic talents and strengths.

- Provide tutoring for any subject in which your child is unable to keep up with the daily demand.

- Have your child take preparation classes for the SAT, the ACT, and college admission tests.

- Allow your child to take driver's education with obtaining a license as a goal. Many AD/HD students and their families put this off a year or two until the student's maturation level is more appropriate for this responsibility.

- Decide on the type of higher education or vocational pursuit.

- Involve your child with a part-time job based on her individual strengths.

- Guide your child in sexual planning.

College and Beyond:

- Understand the American Disabilities Act (ADA) and how it may affect a job in the future.

- Find a college that offers accommodations for the AD/HD student.

- Encourage your young adult to attend marriage and family planning sessions.

- Learn about graduate school accommodations.

- Learn about workplace accommodations.

The Family that Succeeds with AD/HD

What makes a family with children with attention disorders successful? Every family can find their own individual ways to achieve the life they envision. Dr. Stephen Covey is internationally known for his inspirational messages for successful adults. His book *The Seven Habits of Highly Effective People* offers ideas for developing a high-functioning standard of living. I adapt his "Seven Habits" format in Figure 4-2 and offer seven lifestyle behaviors that families with children with AD/HD will want to consider developing as their habits.

Figure 4-2:
The Seven Habits of Highly Effective Parents of AD/HD Children*

1 Have a good sense of humor

2 Understand what AD/HD is & how it effects the child

3 Are involved with the school process

4 Are aware of laws protecting their child

5 Make creative efforts

6 Select appropriate resources

7 Provide unconditional love

(* With respect to Dr. Stephen Covey's *The Seven Habits of Highly Effective People* 1990)

Good parenting takes spirit, dedication, and hard work, and the parent of a child with an attention deficit disorder will work even harder than most. The good news is that parents do not have to "reinvent the wheel." There are multiple techniques and interventions to assist them. From materials to research to support groups, the dedicated parent will find a path to follow. Families seeking the answers to understanding this disorder will find that consistent dedication to goals and plans will impact its path.

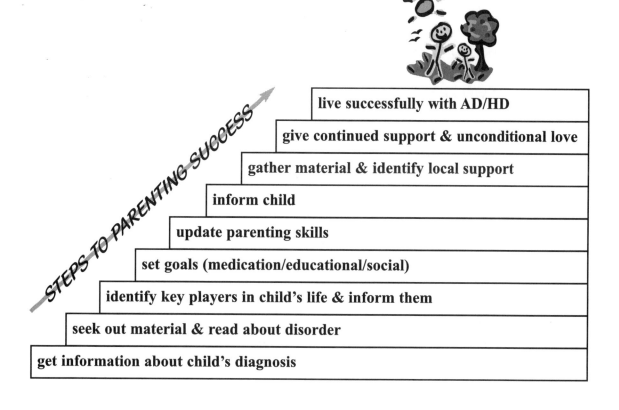

STEPS TO PARENTING SUCCESS

- live successfully with AD/HD
- give continued support & unconditional love
- gather material & identify local support
- inform child
- update parenting skills
- set goals (medication/educational/social)
- identify key players in child's life & inform them
- seek out material & read about disorder
- get information about child's diagnosis

Immediate Resources for Families

Here are some direct resources families can begin to use. Professionals can guide parents to see these resources as part of their support system.

- **Public Library**
  The public library offers a multitude of books, magazines, pamphlets, and video materials in the area of attention disorder. Many libraries today also offer Internet access.

- *Catalog*

  This free catalog offers numerous materials, books, and resources available for purchase. They are often helpful for developing new ideas.

    The A.D.D. Warehouse Catalog
    1-800-233-9273
    www.addwarehouse.com

- *Support Groups*

  There are numerous support groups offered in every state. The largest support group CHADD (Children and Adults with Attention-Deficit/Hyperactivity Disorder) has a toll free number and a hot line to answer questions. They have monthly live Internet talks featuring experts in the field.

    CHADD
    1-800-233-4050
    www.chadd.org

- *Magazines*

  These magazines are available at local bookstores, by subscription, or through membership.

ADDitude *Magazine*	*Attention! Magazine*
1-800-856-2032	(a publication of CHADD
www.additudemag.com	offered with membership)
	1-800-233-4050
	www.chadd.org

- *Internet Chat Groups*

  The ADDvisor Chat Group, <*www.ADDvisor@yahoogroups.com*>, features regular chats about AD/HD with experts in the field.

- *Internet Question and Answer Formats*

  The web page <*www.additudemag.com*>, provided by *ADDitude Magazine*, has four experts answering questions monthly on AD/HD. I am featured as the learning expert.

> *"Attention disorders are chronic, but fortunately, a wide array of drugs is available to effectively treat the disorder."*
>
> —Martin L. Korn, M.D., 2001

Making the Move toward Using Medication

The most effective treatment for people who have attention deficit disorder, with or without hyperactivity, is carefully fine-tuned medication (Brown 1999). The parents and physician may choose medication as part of the multi-modality treatment. It is, no doubt, one of the most difficult decisions a parent will have to make about the plan; however, it can be one of the most successful interventions. Over 36 years of study regarding these medications still indicate they are the most important part of the intervention plan. The medication helps to stabilize brain functions to the point that these children are on the same playing field as their peers, enabling them to concentrate better and longer (Cooley 2002). The medication is not used to control and fix the child's behavior; rather it is used to improve the symptoms of the attention deficit. It is important that the family be educated and well-informed when medication is a chosen course of action. Once they recognize that their child has a disorder that makes part of his brain function differently and that the disorder may respond to a medication, they can begin to understand what medication does to help normalize some of these brain functions.

The choices of medications that support AD/HD symptoms are psychostimulants. They are generally considered safe medications with very few concerns about their use when well-monitored by the physician. Stimulants have been an important support for the majority of children and adults who struggle with AD/HD. At least 80% of AD/HD diagnosed children respond to one of the stimulants if they are tried in a systematic manner (AMA Guidelines, page 1037). A new study conducted by scientists at the National Institute of Mental Health followed children who have been on medication during the past ten years. This study found no evidence that the medicines routinely prescribed for the disorder have reduced brain volume or led to brain damage. The federal researchers said that over time, no obvious defects or evidence of cell damage were apparent in children who used these medications (Talan, 2002). Once parents have read initial information about the disorder, they may want to confer with their own medical expert (physician, nurse practitioner, or psychiatrist) about the pros and cons of psychostimulant therapy.

The American Medical Academy has written specific treatment guidelines for physicians working with families who have a child with attention deficit. The AMA presented these standards for treatment, considered to be the "best practice guidelines," to physicians in January of 2001. The guidelines state that it is the physician's role to recommend medication as one part of the treatment plan and that the physician is to include suggestions for behavior therapy techniques and interventions as the other part of the plan. The guidelines also suggest that primary care clinicians should establish a management program for the child. These guidelines insure that a team effort is an integral part of a working plan for success.

> *"The long-term care of a child with AD/HD requires an ongoing partnership among clinicians, parents, teachers, and the child. Other school personnel – nurses, psychologists, and counselors – can also help with developing and monitoring plans."*
>
> (AMA Guidelines, page 1036)

Side Effects

Psychostimulants are all taken orally with the exception of the newly designed "patch" which is worn on the body. Appetite suppression and weight loss are common side effects from these medications. These side effects may originally have a slight affect on height and weight, but studies of stimulant use suggest that there is little or no growth delay. Recognizing that these two side effects may cause concern for some children, physicians will carefully monitor food intake and sleep habits. Parents will want to offer the child healthy food choices, including protein for breakfast and carbohydrates in the afternoon and evening. This diet management may help the appetite suppression. Reduction of sugar and caffeine will also be helpful.

Some children may experience a "rebound" effect when they are off the medication at the end of the day. They will appear more active than previously observed. Supportive techniques to encourage sleep include having a white sound box on at bedtime, a wind-down period between active evening and bedtime, warm milk, and nightly rituals.

The most serious, though fairly infrequent, side effect can be the unmasking of latent tics or involuntary motor movements such as clearing of the throat, eye blinking, and repeated opening of the mouth. Generally the tic will disappear when the medication is stopped.

Figure 5-1, below and on page 56, describes commonly used medications and notes possible positive and negative results.

Figure 5-1: Typical Medications Prescribed for AD/HD

Drug Class: Psychostimulants

Common Names: Ritalin, Ritalin QD, Dexedrine, Adderall, Adderall XR*, Concerta*, Metadent*, MethyPatch, Cylert**

Possible Positive Effects:
increases attention
controls impulsiveness
reduces task-irrelevant behaviors
may increase compliance
may improve writing
enhances short-term memory

Possible Negative Effects:
may reduce appetite
may result in slight growth delay
may result in mild insomnia
may cause tics

Drug Class: Tricyclic Antidepressants

Common Names: Tofanil, Norpramin, Effexor XR, Anafranil

Possible Positive Effects:
increases attending behavior
increases verbality and gestures
may reduce depression and anxiety
decreases disruptive behavior

Possible Negative Effects:
may affect cardiovascular function
dry mouth
constipation

Figure 5-1: Typical Medications Prescribed for AD/HD, *continued*

Drug Class: **Aminoketones**

Common Name: Wellbutrin

Possible Positive Effects: may reduce hyperactivity
has slight affect on attention
may reduce aggression

Possible Negative Effects: may cause headaches
constipation
seizures

Drug Class: **Antihypertensives**

Common Name: Clonidine

Possible Positive Effects: reduces hyperactivity
reduces impulsivity
decreases aggressive behavior

Possible Negative Effects: may trigger delirium and hallucinations
may cause fall in blood pressure
may cause mood disorder

---

* This medication is taken with food and lasts approximately 12.5 hours.
** This medication is rarely used due to its potential for side effects affecting liver function.

(Pharmaceutical Research and Manufacturers of America 2002 and Jones 1998)

Note: Scientists have developed a new medication that is the first non-stimulant medication for attention disorder. Results from a study published in *The Journal of Pediatrics* (January, 2002) suggest that the medicine reduces inattention and impulsivity. Developed by scientists at Eli Lilly, the chemical has been given the technical name Atomoxetine. It targets two chemicals in the brain - dopamine and norepinephrine. It should be on the market in spring of 2003.

How Does Medication Work?

Messages are sent along the electrical pathways of the brain much like a computer network. The axon (a hair-like fiber attached to a neuron) of one cell plugs into the dendritic spine of another cell, similar to the way an electrical plug connects to the wall socket. In the brains of people with attention disorder, the plug doesn't go all the way in, creating a small gap (called a synaptic gap) between the axon and the dendrite spine. When an electrical pulse (message) comes along the neurotubule (the pathway for the neuron) to the brain, it cannot get across the synaptic gap without chemicals called neurotransmitters. These neurotransmitters, which are carried through brain cells by vesicle balls, form a bridge, allowing the message to cross the gap. The three neurotransmitters most commonly linked to AD/HD are dopamine, serotonin, and norepinephrine. The chemical dopamine is really the most important and must be in the gap for this process to work.

Stimulant medication appears to work by burning glucose which keeps the message-carrying dopamine neurotransmitter in the synaptic gap longer, thus allowing the message to continue on its way. The longer dopamine is in the gap, the stronger the circuit is on which the message travels. Figure 5-2 illustrates how medication helps brain cells make the connection.

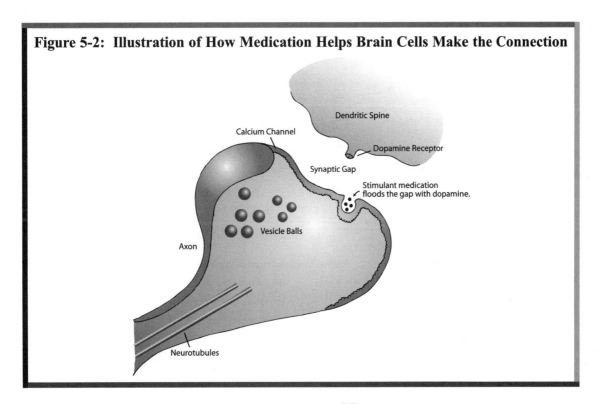

Figure 5-2: Illustration of How Medication Helps Brain Cells Make the Connection

Specific Dose

There is no consistent relationship between weight, height, or age and clinical response to the medication (CHADD 1999). Therefore, the physician must determine the exact dose for each child by observing the results of the medication. Physicians may use a "blind placebo" test (a trial of medication) which helps determine the most beneficial dosage. The child takes a different dose of medication each week for a period of three weeks: a "fake" pill, a lower dose of medication, and a higher dose of medication. Parents and teachers complete rating scales and then compare them at the end of the three weeks. The ideal dosage is the medicine taken during the week that the child's behaviors and learning were most improved. The physician can also choose to start a trial with a low dosage and then gradually increase the medication dosage based on the results of the parent and teacher checklists.

The Results of the Medication

Research indicates that children who take medication for the symptoms of AD/HD attribute their successes to themselves, not to the medication. Parents and teachers may observe that these medications will impact or reduce hyperactive behavior, fidgeting, or active movement. They might also note an improvement in the child's focus for writing. The child may see such an increase in focus that he is able to copy faster from board to paper and from book to paper. We frequently see the most dramatic effects in handwriting. The result may be a more concise and better-formed handwriting. As mentioned on page 33, handwriting samples taken before and after medication will visually portray the results of the medication.

> *"After one week on the medication, I noticed I was able to read a book for longer and longer periods. My interest was sustained and I actually completed a book for the first time. In the past I had only scanned books. I was reading!"* —High school sophomore with AD/HD

Some children or adults taking the medication may detect that they are able to sustain their attention for a longer period of time. They will most often notice this in reading assignments. They often state they are more aware of what they are reading and can relate to what they have just read. Others will not be aware of any differences until you point them out. Because so many of the AD/HD behaviors impact social awareness, the differences AD/HD people exhibit when they are on medication are frequently noticed first by the people working with or around them.

> *"The difference on medication for my daughter was overwhelming. I felt like I finally was able to see how delightful she could be."* —Mother of a hyperactive nine-year-old female

Pills Plus Skills

The effects of this medication will not eliminate habits the child has developed that are learned behaviors. The medication cannot give the child information he has not learned. However, if a new behavior is taught as a replacement or substitute for an old behavior, the child will learn and retain the new behavior. If a new task is taught and the child successfully employs the task, the chances are positive that this is what he will remember. The success of medicine depends on skills, tools, and self-recognition. The statement "pills plus skills" is an effective way to remember that the true success of medication is when both of the interventions work together.

Checklists

After the child has been on the medicine for about a week, parents need to ask the child's teachers to complete checklists. These commercially-offered checklists provide opportunities for the teachers to note their observations of the child on medication. The teacher is a keen observer as to the results of this medication for the child within a group situation. In addition, should the dosage be insufficient or too high, we can expect that the teacher will be one of the first to observe this effect. The completed checklists should then be shared with the physician to determine if the dosage is appropriate. Figure 5-3, page 60, lists some behaviors children on medication may display.

Figure 5-3: Typical Observations on Medication

Too Much Medication	Appropriate Amount of Medication	Not Enough Medication
reduced cognitive response	normal or more alert response	no change
drooling	reduction of verbal mediations	active
dazed or lifeless look	alert, eye contact	inattentive
sleepy	cognitive vigor	impulsive

Note: If the child's reaction is severe hyperactivity or overt chaotic behavior, the reaction is not appropriate and parents should contact the physician immediately regarding discontinuing the medicine.

Explaining the Medication to the Child

Once a medication has been decided on, the parents or caregivers need to sit down with the child and explain what they have learned from the evaluator and what the purpose of the medication is. Parents should introduce the information in a positive manner, stating that they have learned that the child's testing indicated that he has difficulty with attention and focus and that this challenge may be helped by taking a medication. They should help the child understand that this is something his doctor feels will make a difference. Parents need to explain that this medication should make a change in the child's focus and, with that change, he should experience greater understanding of schoolwork. Therefore, over the long-term, stronger memory ability may occur. Parents also need to encourage the child to ask questions about the medication.

Taken alone, medication is not enough to help a child with attention disorder difficulties achieve continued success. Therefore, a critical part of the conversation should be that even though this particular medication will help the child focus better and pay attention, it will not be effective if the child does not continue to work as hard as he can. Reinforce this important statement to the child, **"This medication will not work unless you do!"** This statement is critical because the child needs to realize that he is working *with* the medication.

One way to refer to the medication is to suggest it is a *tool*. It is helpful to use examples the child may identify with, such as glasses are a tool to help someone read, a hearing aid is a tool to help someone hear, and a wheelchair is a tool to help someone get around. Indicate how these tools offer support to people and how the use of a *medication tool* is similar. Parents need to understand that it is very important **not** to refer to the medication as a "fix-it pill," a "smart pill," or a "vitamin." Instead, they should truthfully explain what it can and cannot do.

There are several books about medicine for children and young adults. They include *Otto Takes his Medicine, Putting on the Brakes, Shelly the Hyperactive Turtle, Eagle Eyes,* and *First Star I See.* Contact the A.D.D. Warehouse at 1-800-233-9273 for a catalog listing these books.

Ten Frequently-Asked Questions about Medication

1 I'm worried about putting my child on medication. What does the research say about the medication? *This medication has been researched for over 50 years. When correctly used and monitored, it is a very safe and effective therapy for attention disorders.*

2 How long will my child be on the medication? Should he stop taking it when he reaches puberty? *Most children are on the medication for several years. 80% of the children will continue to need the medication as teenagers, and 50% will continue to need the medication as adults. The medication should be taken through puberty. There are no medical reasons why this medication would be affected by puberty, so there is no reason to stop it at this time.*

3 Should my child be off the medication on weekends and summer vacation? *Dr. Larry Silver, a physician in Bethesda, MD, and nationally known for his work with the medication, recommends that if the child is learning skills and participating in activities that require focus and recall, he is best-served by remaining on the medication all seven days of the week. If a child is losing some weight on the medication and is planning a weekend or a vacation with no real demands, then this would be a good time to stop the medication for a short period. Consistent taking of the medication results in stronger success for the child.*

4 What side effects may occur? *Some children will have a reduced appetite and may lose weight. Less than 2% of the children initially experience a slower growth rate, but regain their normal growth by age 18. Some children experience difficulty sleeping and winding down in the evening. A small percentage develops tic disorders. These tics include vocal tics such as clearing of the throat and motor tics such as blinking. When the medication stops, the tic stops; however, many people feel the merit of the medication is such that they are willing to put up with the tic.*

5 How long will it take before we see a difference in our child on the medication? *If the child is doing a task which requires extended independent focus such as copying from board to paper, reading a story that requires response to comprehension questions, or completing a writing task that requires sustained attention, you may be able to see a difference as soon as 45 minutes after the dosage.*

6 Since I am giving the medicine at home and it lasts all day, is it necessary for me to tell the school that my child is on medication? *Your child's medication can be confidential information if the school is not involved with the dosage. However, I believe you are involved with a team process and the school should be a part of the team. For example, if the child should be randomly drug tested or if there should be any side effects that may be exhibited during the school day, it is critical that someone knows about your child's medicine. In addition, the physician will want the teacher to observe and report on behaviors closely so they can determine proper dosage and efficiency. Without the teacher's participation, this valuable insight and information would not be available to you.*

7 My child is unable to take the long-term medications; therefore, he needs to take his medication at school. Who will give it to him since we do not have a school nurse? *The laws protecting children taking medication in school mandate that a designated administrative person gives the medication. Work with your school personnel to determine who this person will be. The principal will often take over this responsibility or assign a specific person to do it. Be sure that there is also a responsible backup to take over this duty in case the selected person is ever absent.*

8 Will my child abuse other drugs because he takes this drug? *Because stimulant drugs are also drugs of abuse, you should be rightfully concerned. While stimulants clearly have abuse potential, research indicates that the rate of lifetime, non-medical, methylphenidate use has not significantly increased since this was introduced as a treatment for AD/HD (Goldman et al. 1998, Swanson 1999). Research indicates that children who understand what their medications are for and how they are used do not abuse them. Students who have symptoms of AD/HD but go untreated, may abuse other substances in an attempt to self-medicate themselves.*

9 How can we as a family help our child feel positive about his medication? *Treat the medicine and the child with respect. Make sure the child realizes that it is his hard work in conjunction with the medicine that is making a difference. When success is noted, give credit to the child, NOT the medicine. Here is an example of a positive and a negative way to respond.* **Positive Response:** *"You are really doing a super job with concentration. I saw how you reviewed your notes and underlined them. That certainly helps."* **Negative Response:** *"You are a much better student now that you take medication."*

10 My child is whiny and fussy at the end of the day on medicine. It certainly helps him during the day but we are concerned about his mood when he comes home. What can we do? *Talk with the doctor about the dosage and what occurs at different times of the day. Some children experience a rebound effect as the medicine wears off. Often a change in dosage can make a difference. Also be sure your child is drinking enough water everyday. It can also be helpful to have your child start the day with protein-based foods rather than a sugar or carbohydrate breakfast. Offer and encourage carbohydrates in the evening. These nutritional suggestions can help to balance the effect of the glucose burning medication.*

> *"Although medication will help many children with AD/HD to focus and concentrate better, structuring the home environment and using rewards and punishment consistently will help keep the child on track. The key word for any behavioral program is consistency!"*
>
> —H. Russell Searight, Ph.D., 1999

All children appear at times to be impulsive or hyperactive. Children diagnosed with attention deficit, however, experience these symptoms every day. They encounter this conflict everywhere—on the ball field, at school, in a shopping center, in an elevator, on a playground, etc. In brief, it is constant in their lives and it becomes a part of the lives of their families. When their symptoms are managed, these children are in tune with the world, but when the symptoms are not managed, the children are out of sync. This active behavior often makes them socially inappropriate or unacceptable to others. Parents of AD/HD children in my practice often share how their children are not included in peer birthday parties, neighborhood group activities, and team sports. They relate that their children's actions reduce their acceptance in their schools and neighborhood communities. This lack of inclusion can be embarrassing or hurtful to a family and to siblings who may not experience the same disorder.

It is helpful to remember that every family is unique. Parents of AD/HD children need to avoid judging themselves based on other family's behaviors. They need to remember that *different is not defective*. Parents of an AD/HD child will want to be their child's advocate. Not everyone will understand the child's behavior and these people may question their parenting techniques. Parents need to be informed, know what techniques work best with AD/HD children, and attempt to stay committed to the behavior strategies they select. They need to ignore ill-intentioned and uninformed observers and seek friendships with families who understand what they are doing and why.

Effective parenting of a child with attention disorders presents stress and challenge for most families. The mere description of the disorder's essential characteristics (inattention, impulsivity, and hyperactivity) projects images of misunderstanding, disappointment, and concern. Couple the disorder with the very real probability that it co-exists with other disorders and we can understand why parents of children with AD/HD may be frustrated by their parenting attempts. To implement a successful behavior plan for children with AD/HD, parents need a good understanding of the behaviors that are a part of their child's disorder and a strong behavior modification program.

Life Span Disorder

Attention deficit is a life-span disorder (i.e., it will continue for the duration of a person's life). The symptoms may change over their life spans, but children will not outgrow attention disorders. The preschooler who is constantly on the go becomes the fidgety, elementary student who develops into the restless adolescent who grows into the multi-task orientated, stimulus-seeking adult. Figure 6-1 illustrates characteristic behaviors in the life of an AD/HD child.

Figure 6-1: Growing Up AD/HD

PRESCHOOL	ELEMENTARY	ADOLESCENCE
➤ Displays intense activity	➤ Is fidgety	➤ Is restless
➤ Exhibits uncontrolled talking	➤ Talks excessively	➤ Talks out without regard to situation or place
➤ Displays a beginning resistance to order and routines	➤ Shows inconsistent performance	➤ Has problems at school
➤ Is aggressive in play	➤ Is bossy, not a team player	➤ Seems immature
➤ Is egocentric	➤ Displays a constant demand for attention	➤ Is not responsible
➤ Has a demanding personality	➤ Appears careless	➤ Shows poor judgment
		➤ Is considered a high risk for auto accidents

(Levine 1993 and Jones 1994)

Co-Morbidity

Attention deficit/hyperactivity impulsive disorder is often associated with the development of other disruptive disorders, in particular conduct and oppositional-defiant disorder. Researchers do not know why this occurs. They speculate that the impulsivity and heedlessness of the disorder interfere with social learning or with close social bonds with parents in a way that predisposes to the development of behavior disorders (Barkley 1998). Children may begin to show the signs of these disorders as early as age six. By the time they reach young adulthood, approximately 65% of the teenagers are also diagnosed with oppositional defiant disorder (ODD) and 45% are diagnosed with Conduct Disorder (CD).

It is important to remember that no disorder remains alone. They often cluster with other disorders, thus presenting a co-occurrence of multiple challenges. Children with the **highest** levels of hyperactivity appear to be at the greatest risk for the multiple behavior symptoms. Typical co-morbid (co-occurring) influences with AD/HD include depression, anxiety, oppositional defiant disorder, and possibly Tourette's syndrome. In addition, obsessive-compulsive disorder and bipolar disorder may also be noted. When these co-occurring disorders are present, the treatment plan will be more complex and require additional support for the child and family. The differences in these disorders need to be identified by a professional in order to prescribe additional or different medication and to add further treatment suggestions to the child's regimen. Figure 6-2 demonstrates the occurrence of co-morbidity within the attention deficit population.

Figure 6-2: Co-Morbidity

Complication	% of Occurrence in AD/HD Population	Behaviors Observed
Depression	11%	• experiences changes in sleep patterns, eating, and energy • has low motivation • is not interested in same things • is indecisive
Anxiety and Mood Disorders	25%	• worries • has muscle tension • is fearful of new situations • is irritable
Oppositional Defiant Disorder	40% to 50%	• shows disrespect for adult authority • loses temper, is touchy, shows anger • argues, annoys, is spiteful
Conduct Disorder	25%	• bullies and initiates fights • can be physically cruel to people and/or animals • may be involved in setting fires • destroys property
Learning Disability	33%	• has deficits in reading, math, language, or written expression
Bipolar	20%	• shows psychotic symptoms • has gross distortions in reality • has impaired thought processes • throws severe temper tantrums • is more irritable in the morning • is aggressive and destructive • exhibits pronounced sexual activity • giggles loudly
Tic Disorders	25% to 75%	• has tic syndromes including Tourette's, clearing of the throat, eye twitches, and shaking of the head • has verbal outbursts
Communication Disorders	6% to 35%	• has pragmatic deficits • stutters • has problem-solving deficits • has auditory and language processing deficits

(Teeter 1998 and Barkley 1998)

69

Who Wants to Play with a Hyperactive Child?

Impulsive behavior affects how a child interacts with others. A child with AD/HD may initially appear engaging to others. But, when these people realize the child is not willing to listen to them or to take turns, they will not remain friends with the child. People perceive an impulsive person as uncaring and reckless.

Parents can help the AD/HD child learn appropriate social skills by modeling accepted behaviors. At home, parents should put emphasis on the rehearsal of good manners and reward situations where the child has demonstrated skillful controlled social interaction. Parents should seek resources in the community that offer classes in social skills, etiquette, and how to manage different social situations. These types of classes are often offered in the summer at camps and at therapeutic care centers.

Parents need to find activities and social events where their child can feel accepted. The child with attention difficulties will respond best to activities that are short, have variety, and offer well-structured routines and order. The goal is to start slow by introducing games and tasks that are brief and have a clear end in sight. Select diversions that have a simple format, but incorporate variety. Gradually introduce games that offer concentration and help increase attention and patience.

Prior to entering the child into group activities, role-play possible difficult situations she might experience in group interaction activities. Act out how to take turns, what to do if someone pushes, and what to do if you win or lose. Provide on-going and immediate feedback as you play with your child. For example, say, "I can see that you know how to take turns. Your friends will want you on their team because you take turns." It is wise to use physical modeling as a cue to taking a turn. Place your open palm on your chest for "my turn" and hold out your open palm to your child for "her turn."

Play can also involve crafts, hobbies, and collecting things. The child who begins to collect certain items and display them in a book, box, or case learns order, classification, comparison, and categorization. Hobbies can reinforce skills or tolerance, such as patience, order, or saving to buy a specific object.

Following are some typical activities that can be successful for AD/HD children along with some suggestions on how to accommodate the child for each activity.

Team Sports

By nature, AD/HD children are not team players. Their limited attention makes it hard for them to wait for a turn. They do best in sports that allow individuals a chance to excel on their own. If a child has some athletic ability, explore sports that are more individual. Consider golf, tennis, gymnastics, wrestling, martial arts (particularly Tai Kwan Do), bowling, water or snow skiing, swimming, and diving. If the child has a desire to play a team sport, help her choose a position where she will be most active or will be involved with the ball most frequently.

Musical Experiences

Children with attention deficits frequently have difficulty with visual motor integration. This means it is harder for them to remember what they have just seen or heard and then write it down. This motor-memory challenge will impede the AD/HD child's music-reading skills. Guide your child's music interest by selecting musical instruments where she can see the notes on the music sheet and her fingers at the same time. This is possible in instruments, such as the trumpet, clarinet, and drums. Playing the piano requires visual motor memory to read the notes and memorize key combinations. Successful AD/HD pianists often play by ear, not by reading the notes.

Creative Areas

Many successful adults with AD/HD are employed in creative arts fields, such as visual graphics, visual arts, the theatre, television, and journalism. These resilient adults have learned that their verbal skills and/or artistic traits are assets in these vocations. Give your AD/HD child an opportunity to try drama classes, children's theater, debates, and speech classes. Art and sketching classes as well as animation and cartoon drawing classes may also be helpful and appeal to your child's strengths.

Magic

Learning magic and performing magic tricks are positive play experiences for many distracted children. They thrill to the variety of doing a trick and are delighted with the special recognition it brings to them. Magic is an individually taught skill, and it provides the child the opportunity to develop a talent rather than be involved in a competitive experience. The child moves forward in magic as she develops and personally acquires the skill. This self-paced learning activity compliments the typical AD/HD child's learning strengths.

Chess

This individual sport offers a unique experience to use big picture thinking—something AD/HD people often possess. It provides rehearsal for observing details and aids in building personal skills, such as turn taking and strategy planning. Chess players are matched with others of like skill so there is no age barrier. It can provide participants with an incentive-based reward system because players gradually move up in levels based on their skills.

Board Games

You will need to help the AD/HD child with turn-taking skills when playing a board game. Have the children pass a colorful Koosh ball back and forth between turns. The children can quickly determine whose turn it is by who is holding the ball. Here are some games you can try with your child: Milton Bradley games *Electronic Simon*, *Memory*, *Guess Who?*, *Twister*, and *Connect Four*; *Somebody* by Aristoplay; pick-up sticks; self-contained plastic mazes; and pinball games.

Incompetence vs. Non-compliance

Dr. Sam Goldstein, a leading specialist in attention deficit, stresses that parents of AD/HD children must recognize the difference between incompetence and non-compliance. *Incompetence* is the lack of a skill, tool, or strategy to control an action. For example, most AD/HD children have difficulty copying from book to paper. They have documented difficulties with this skill, and their lack of focus reduces their success with this task. For them to be successful with this task, they need training, guidance, and tools. No amount of punishment will change this behavior; it is one that must be learned. If the parent reacts by punishing the child every time she fails to copy effectively in a timely manner, the child will soon respond negatively. Goldstein describes *non-compliance* as when children know what their parents are suggesting, but choose not to comply. For example, a parent says to his child, "Jason, I want you to come in now. It's seven o'clock." Jason responds by riding away on his bike. Jason understood his parent's request and yet chose not to follow it. When this occurs, parents should respond with immediate consequences.

It is important for parents of children with attention concerns to know what areas could be areas of incompetence for their children. Recognizing incompetence is a step toward developing tools for coping with the disorder. The evaluation process and assessment may provide specific information as to what a child knows and does not know. Some areas of incompetent behavior often noted in children with AD/HD are listed in Figure 6-3, page 74, along with suggestions for training and support.

Figure 6-3: Dealing with Incompetence

Incompetence:	Suggestions for training and support:
Difficulty following multiple-step directions	• Give brief directions. • Ask the child to repeat what you said or act it out. • Give directions in list form on white board or paper and have the child cross out each direction as she completes it. • Help the child learn to highlight written directions with a colored pen. • Hold up one finger as you state each step. This gives the child visual cues to associate with the steps of a direction.
Completing tasks in a timely manner	• Use a timer for some tasks, allowing the child to estimate how long it will take her to complete the task. • Help the child make a plan to accomplish the task. • Offer an incentive for completing a task. ("If you do this, this will happen.")
Recall of rote details	• Help the child memorize using mnemonics or other cues and tricks to recall details. For example, use a rap tape to teach math facts rather than using flash cards repeatedly. • Let the child see unique and different items. Then try to apply them to what is same and similar. • Use color when teaching details. For example, when teaching capitalization, highlight all the capitals in one color. Teach the child to continue this.
Copying and writing	• Let your child have more time to copy. • Number the items to be copied and highlight certain words. This will "cue" the child and make copying more productive for her. • Break writing activities into chunks or small assignments. • Encourage your child to learn keyboard skills so she can develop typing as a compensatory skill.

Successful Behavior Strategies with AD/HD Children

Parents of a child with AD/HD need to evoke consistent follow-through and predictable rewards and punishment. All adults who interact with the child will need to agree on strategies and present a united front. First, they need to be sure the child understands the desired behavior. AD/HD children will need a cue to alert them when their behavior begins to escalate. These children will react to a rehearsed pre-determined cue as a reminder to extinguish a behavior. Parents should create "cues" that include nonverbal hand signals along with a verbal comment. For example, when asking the child to stop talking, accompany the verbal request with the hand signal of one finger across the lips. Then recheck the child's understanding by having her repeat the auditory information. There are numerous materials to help parents with these interventions including the excellent resource *1-2-3 Magic: Training Your Children to Do What You Want!* by Tom Phelan.

At home, many parents of AD/HD children find success when they carefully plan a daily schedule for the family to follow. Daily schedules should include expected times for transitions, routines, and rituals. Parents can plan dinner at the same time every night, schedule designated times for television watching, and encourage a quiet time spent before bed. The child's environment at home should be safe and well-maintained. Order and routine provide calmness and stability to an active, impulsive child. Toys and belongings need to be in drawers, in boxes, or on shelves. Parents need to circulate toys, bringing out only a few at a time to maintain the child's alertness and interests. To help the child begin to remember where items should be kept, label and color-code personal belongings.

Figure 6-4, page 76, is a summary of a variety of behavior strategies that have proven highly successful for the management of active, impulsive children. These behavior strategies are explained in more detail on pages 77-81.

Figure 6-4: Successful Behavior Strategies with AD/HD Children

a) **Positive Reinforcement**—the use of rewards, privileges, and verbal praise contingent on the child's behavior.

b) **Contracts**—child and parent create a written document, which details what behavior is expected and what consequences will exist if contract is not fulfilled.

c) **Token Program**—use of tokens earned for performing expected behaviors. Child turns in tokens for desired privileges.

d) **Response Cost**—removal of rewards, points, tokens, or privileges based on inappropriate behavior.

e) **Redirection**—the technique of redirecting (refocusing) the child's behavior to another activity.

f) **Time-out**—removal from situation thus eliminating child from activity. Based on short attention span, the time will differ for each child to remain in the time-out chair. Consider one minute for each year of life.

g) **List-Making**—parents make a short list for the child to accomplish during homework or chore time. Use a white board and write the items in color. Start by listing three items, increasing the number as the child is able to handle them. The child will cross off each item as she completes it. Gradually encourage the child to add to the list and eventually create her own itemized list.

a) **Positive Reinforcement**—Children with attention deficit often exhibit low self-esteem based on their personal experiences with the disorder. They are so often criticized and corrected that they begin to wonder what they can do right. Dr. Sam Goldstein, a respected psychologist, speculates that about 80% of their day is negative comments from others about their performance and behavior. Parents and professionals need to use specific positive feedback and reinforcement when working with these students. These children profit from immediate reinforcement, such as coupons, points, cards, and tokens. They respond well to visual cues, so positive body language like the thumbs-up gesture, a wink, a smile, and a generally upbeat expression will fortify them. Verbal praise must be specific and include what they did that was right. Tell them the benefit of their actions. Offer thanks and encourage them for future success. They respond well to corrective feedback if it is clear and concise in its manner. It is critical that parents and providers back up their statements with action and avoid sarcasm at all cost.

b) **Making a Contract**—A written contract can also be a tool to help parents manage their child's inappropriate behavior. The parents and child write a contract regarding the behavior that needs to be changed. For example, a parent may want the child to stop using a negative word. The parent writes the contract in the child's presence stating what the behavior is, what needs to be changed, and what the result or reward will be if the child successfully modifies the behavior. The parent also lists a consequence if the behavior is not extinguished. All parties sign the contract. The parent posts the contract in a prominent place such as on the kitchen refrigerator or on a family bulletin board. When all parties feel the desired behavior has been accomplished, the contract has been completed and can be destroyed.

c) **Token Programs**—AD/HD children respond well to a highly visual, consistent behavior program based on tangible immediate rewards. A token system using small hands-on materials like poker chips, pennies, buttons, or plastic discs is instrumental in working with children with attention disorders. Accomplished behaviors receive a payoff in token form. For example, the child receives three tokens for brushing her teeth, seven tokens for making her bed, and ten tokens for doing her homework without complaining. The child then "trades in" her tokens for specific privileges and rewards. Each family determines a *Menu of Reinforcers* that lists the rewards and privileges and the "cost" for each. The child may pay five tokens to watch a video of her choice, two tokens to sit in a specific chair in the family room while watching TV, or fifteen tokens to go to library. If you use this technique with several children in the family, be sure the tokens are color-coded to prevent one child from taking her sibling's tokens.

It is important that the child receives the tokens as the behavior occurs and that she has a place to store the tokens. The reward must be given when promised. Failing to remember to give the child the reward when the tokens are redeemed will dramatically reduce the effect of the program. Research indicates the token system is highly effective because it offers an immediate response for the child. When the program is unsuccessful, it tends to be because parents do not keep up with the program, forget what to do, or fail to provide immediate rewards. When parents choose to try the token technique, they need to maintain it, believe in its purpose, and stay with it without fail.

d) **Response Cost**—This strategy is helpful in curbing impulsive behavior in a home or group setting and is also effective in the classroom as it can reduce off-task behavior and improve compliance. The AD/HD child needs immediate recognition that the behavior she displayed was inappropriate. The response cost strategy punishes inappropriate behavior by removing something the child possesses or has earned. It is typically used with tangible items, such as points, tokens, or stickers. For example, parents give the child a cluster of tokens to start with. Then, they tell the child that they will take back one token each time they observe negative behavior during a particular period. If there are any tokens left at the end of the time period, the child gets to keep them. The child can then exchange the tokens for predetermined privileges and rewards. To be effective, the child must earn more reinforcers than the parents eliminate. The more points the child accumulates, the greater her chance for reward. Self-control situations where parents might use response cost are a car trip, waiting in line at an amusement park, and taking turns talking in a family conversation.

e) **Redirection**—Redirection is a simple behavior technique that involves ignoring the behavior and redirecting the person to another more appropriate behavior. This strategy can quickly stifle an annoying behavior that needs to be changed. The purpose of redirection is to distract a child from the behavior she is engaged in and direct her to substitute another more positive activity for the behavior. The technique is highly successful with the AD/HD child, young adult, or adult. Because they are so easily distracted, it is easy to get them off topic with redirection. Remember, you can usually distract a highly distractible person!

> *A two-year-old child grabs something the parents would prefer she doesn't touch. She holds on to the object and won't let go. The parents try to get her to put it down, but to no avail. Finally the parents offer* **redirection** *stating, "Look Caitlin, there's a horse outside our window!" Immediately, the two-year-old drops the item and turns to the new stimulus.*

f) **Time-Out**—Time-out is an intervention that temporarily removes children from the attention of adults and other children. The busy, out-of-control child will often need time away from an activity. Sometimes her overt lack of self-control makes it impossible to reason with her or redirect her behavior. At these times, it is best to have a designated time-out or "cool down" area, such as a chair or an area rug.

Always designate the same chair for time-out at home, but use whatever is available in public, including steps or standing in a corner of a busy store. Be sure the chair is in sight of family members and activity. Determine the amount of time the child will spend in the chair by assigning one minute to each year of her life (e.g., a five-year-old child = five minutes). Be sure the child can see a timer or clock even if she can't tell time. This offers a structured beginning and end to the time-out. Give very active children a Koosh ball, Wikki Stix (small, flexible, non-toxic strings), or sandpaper square to hold while they are seated. You may have to stand next to the child initially.

Here is an example of how to use time-out:

1 Observe a negative behavior, such as a child spitting at her sister.

2 State the rule, "No spitting. Spitting means you are going to time-out."

3 Place the child in a chair or in her room. State the rule again, "Remember, we do not spit at others. Time-out is over when the timer rings."

4 The timer rings and the child gets up. State, "I'm glad you are in control again. Finish the game with your sister."

g) **List-Making**—The child with attention deficit will often have difficulty with following directions, completing tasks, and accomplishing activities that are in rote or sequential format. List-making can be a critical tool taught early on. Parents and professionals can make lists on small white boards or on specially assigned colored paper (i.e., a bright purple pad). It is important that the list looks colorful and stands out among other papers.

The activities on the list should first be introduced in a brief format, adding more items as the child becomes successful with the technique. (If the child is under age six and does not read yet, use pictures or illustrations of the tasks.) Teach the child to cross off each completed item. Make sure the list offers variety because the child will easily "tune out" repeated activities. Therefore, each daily list should offer a unique statement or diversion to keep the inattentive child focused and interested in checking out the list.

There are several behaviors that seem consistent and typical to persons with attention deficit disorders. As parents, we need to quickly think of strategies to extinguish these behaviors. The quick tips in Figure 6-5, page 82, can be helpful when you see your child engaged in one of these behaviors.

Figure 6-5: Quick Tips to Behavior Strategies

If your child is not listening . . .
- Establish eye contact.
- Make directions short and to the point.
- Have your child act out or repeat the direction.
- Use focus words, such as "Look here," "1-2-3," and "Turn to me."

If your child is whining . . .
- Don't overreact.
- Avoid taking the whining personally.
- Realize this is your child's mood, not yours.
- Ignore the behavior. Don't challenge it.

If your child is blaming herself . . .
- Redirect. Change the topic.
- Give your child choices and alternatives.
- Avoid pointing out what she should do better.
- Show that everyone makes mistakes.

If your child is feeling helpless . . .
- Give your child responsibility at home.
- Provide an allowance and privileges as incentives.
- Give your child the opportunity to make her own decisions.
- Turn down appeals for help when you know your child can do it.
- Reward and praise your child immediately when she handles a situation.

Set these guidelines for public behavior . . .
- Set guidelines for your child before going out.
- Offer incentives for appropriate behavior.
- Discuss consequences for inappropriate behavior.
- Respond immediately when your child is exhibiting inappropriate behavior.
- Provide cues and modeling for staying with the behavior plan while in public.
- Let your child know what she is doing that is on task and appropriate.

Watch your language . . .
- Avoid sarcasm.
- Be positive.
- Point out what your child does well.
- Guide your child toward making solutions.

Techniques for Coping with Out-of-Control Behavior

The effectiveness of many parenting techniques depends on a variety of factors—the individual child, the parents' ability to apply the intervention consistently, the child's understanding of the intervention, and the rules of the intervention. Parents who successfully manage outbursts of sudden anger and inappropriate behavior have embraced a variety of strategies and techniques that help them feel positive and in control during difficult times. They have gained confidence and feel secure that they know how to effectively avoid the escalation of behavior problems. The following techniques for coping with out-of-control behavior will ensure that parents are prepared for most situations.

Techniques for Coping with Out-of-Control Behavior

- Anticipate. Know the danger signs.

- Catch the behavior early. Distract the child and redirect her.

- Be neutral when the child goes into orbit.

- Label the behavior you observe. Put emphasis on the behavior, not the child. For example, say, "You are going to get too excited. Calm down and take a deep breath."

- Have some "cool-down" interventions available. Give the child a solution, something reliable she can go to. With a small child, it can be as simple as saying, "Come sit on my lap," or putting on soft music while she plays. With an older child, it can be a bag of crafts, a new magazine, a video game, or watching a movie.

- Identify "high stress" periods for the child during the day. High stress times often include mealtime, the start of day, and home-work time. Problem-solve ways to decrease stress during these times. For example, prepare meals earlier in the day, set out clothes and do homework the night before, or get up a half hour earlier than the child.

Every family has "trying times." Although behavior modification techniques and tips can be very effective, there are times when the following suggestions using typical life examples can be most helpful.

➤ *If your child has difficulty sitting still when she is expected to sit*, provide an object for her to hold and touch.

➤ *If your child is challenged by sitting in the car for long periods of time*, provide tapes, videos, and/or handheld games that are only used during car trips. To maintain their appeal, these activities should not be items the child can play with daily at home.

➤ *If your child finds it hard to sit at the dinner table with family*, allow her to eat her meal ahead of time and join the family for dessert or salad only. This gives her a feeling of being part of the family meal, but it does not require her to sit for an extended period. Gradually increase the time with family so the child can eventually tolerate longer seating.

➤ *If your child tries to sleep with you every evening*, offer a reassuring and similar sound in the child's bedroom. Often the restless child cannot sleep alone because she is listening to every noise in the home. She needs to hear a background noise to distract her. Therefore she finds adult breathing a sound of reassurance. Try to substitute for this by offering a white noise box. These sound machines offer sounds from waves on a beach to static, and this can be very helpful.

➤ *If your child has difficulty with behavior in a public place*, review your rules prior to taking her into a public situation. Talk with your child and agree on a reward for good behavior. Review the consequences for non-compliance. Have the child restate the rules in her own words. During your outing, remind the child about the rule in a positive way. If the child accomplishes the desired behavior, be sure to reward her immediately upon leaving the public place. An example of steps to follow in this situation is on the next page.

Anticipate. You have to take your child grocery shopping with you. You know your child has difficulty waiting in line and grabs candy by the cash register.

Review the rule. "When we are in line, keep your hands to yourself. I'd like you to hold my purse while I pay."

Determine a reward. "You wanted to go to the duck pond. If you keep your hands to yourself, we'll stop by the duck pond and feed the ducks."

Review a consequence. "If you take any candy, we won't see the ducks."

Have the child restate the rule and the reward. "Hands to myself. I can feed the ducks if I keep my hands to myself."

Positively state the reward as you shop. "It's great to know we will be feeding the ducks! Do you want to take bread or corn?"

Reward your child immediately. Drive from the grocery store straight to the duck pond. Say, "When you follow the rules, nice things happen."

(From Jones, C. 1998)

"And the Beat Goes On"—Unending Parenting Techniques

In her book *Hyperactive Children Grown Up*, Dr. Gabrielle Weiss surveyed AD/HD adults who were involved in the Canadian Health Care System for the treatment of AD/HD for many years. She asked them what they felt was the most successful part of their treatment plans. The majority responded that the support they felt from their parents is what made the biggest difference in their lives.

Parenting an active or inattentive child can be overwhelming and at times exhausting. Parents often feel like their entire family revolves around this one child's multiple needs. At times like these, parents need some time out to recognize how critical their involvement with the child is and how unconditional their love for their child must be.

There are many parenting techniques that can be of support to parents of AD/HD children. Following is a list of key behavior strategies for parents to remember at home, at school, or in a related service. These strategies target early childhood, elementary school, middle school, and high school.

Parenting Techniques through the Years

Early Childhood Strategies

• Model good manners and greeting skills for the child at every opportunity.

• Introduce music as a calming element and an instructional tool to increase focus.

• Reduce television watching and video game playing.

• Model schedules and list-making using white erase boards and colorful notepads.

• Introduce a token behavior program.

• Encourage a gradual transition to day care. Start with a small one-on-one situation or a small in-home play group; move to a small childcare center with a classroom size of ten or below; gradually increase to a larger group care center; then move on to kindergarten.

- Provide one appropriate object the child may hold and touch as needed. This might be a Wikki-Stix, a Koosh ball, or a small balloon filled with flour or salt. If the child is constantly trying to touch objects and fidget with them when she is expected to stay seated, this will give her fidgety fingers something to hold and wiggle, thus increasing focus and attention.

Elementary School Strategies

- Select a teacher by affective style (look for the "Master" teacher who demonstrates she uses strong visual cues, facial gestures, and enthusiasm in a firm but flexible style).

- Set up ritual homework time every evening. On nights when there is no homework, have the child participate in quiet reading, studying, or review.

- Encourage the development of outside interests which offer order, continuity, and personal self-esteem building.

- Encourage appropriate social participation by modeling and practicing good social skills.

- Require the child to stay with an activity in which she has asked to participate for at least six times (class, lessons, sports, etc.).

Middle School Strategies

- Use one or more alarm clocks for wake up time.

- Make multiple copies of schedules, assignments, and syllabi.

- Provide the child with a watch that has a beeper as a reminder for important appointments, taking medicine on time, etc.

• Continue rituals at bedtime and in the morning.

• Provide support for organizational skills.

• Engage a study buddy or an educational tutor.

• Offer rewards and incentives for good behavior.

• Hold a weekly session to review the child's homework, help her clean out her book bag, and adjust her daily planner.

• Seek a mentor or coach who will give the child emotional support.

High School Strategies

• Look for experience-based class situations. These incorporate a variety of learning styles.

• Encourage cooperative learning activities.

• Continue the ritual homework period.

• Provide help for developing good driving skills.

• Provide compensatory tools (e.g., computer, tape recorder, calculator, minute minders).

• Encourage mentorship, internship, and coaching.

Finally, let's not forget about parents taking care of themselves. The following list offers some much-needed advice on how to handle the stress that inevitably comes with parenting an AD/HD child.

Taking Care of Yourself

➤ Communicate to others the need for occasional quiet time and solitude without feeling guilty.

➤ Make a concentrated effort to manage your time better. List what you want to accomplish each day on a white board, pad of paper, or Post-it notes. Cross off each item as you complete it. Be satisfied if you complete half of the list or two-thirds of it.

➤ Recognize your accomplishments and what your child has accomplished. Intervene on negative thoughts.

➤ Add more humor to your life. Remember funny incidents that happen during the day and share them with your spouse or a friend.

➤ Take care of your own physical needs. Exercise regularly, eat well, and take time to reward yourself for working hard.

"Danny complained about his teacher from day one. He began to not want to get up in the morning and had numerous somatic complaints. We kept telling Danny he needed to try harder to work with his fifth grade teacher. However, when she sent home a note telling us that his constant foot tapping had kept him from succeeding in her class, we began to see it was more her problem than Danny's. We asked the principal to switch teachers at the semester break and all of a sudden it was like we had a new kid. The new teacher understood his need for movement and worked around it, not against it!" —Mother of a fifth grade AD/HD boy

Picture yourself sitting in a room of 30 other people about your age. Now imagine that every time one of these people coughs, speaks, or moves you must turn and look at them. Overwhelming? Head on a pivot? Impossible to handle? This is a very real example of what it might be like for a student with attention deficit in a typical classroom. Every sound or movement draws his attention away from what he is doing. He has no control over tuning these things out, but literally must acknowledge every action. Talk about stimulus overload! Now, add to our hypothetical situation one adult in the room who corrects you every time you turn to a sound or follow a movement. How would YOU react to that amount of correction? Angry? Confused? Defeated? How strong would your self-esteem be?

This anecdote is just a glimpse into the world of the AD/HD student. Children with attention disorders are often not referred for evaluation until they enter the school environment where they are required to demonstrate self-control, focus, and follow-through. They enter the classroom with great expectations but are unable to produce consistent results equal to their classmates. They are unable to cope with the environment and have inefficient skills for developing their own strategies. They appear to need more than the usual amount of cueing, direction, and help to be industrious. Because they are woefully unprepared to meet deadlines, return things in a timely fashion, organize, and plan, their worlds just fall apart.

What the Parent Can Do

It is critical that the parent and the professional work together to devise a successful school environment for the child with attention disorders. Working within the school environment to control attention deficits certainly requires a team effort. The result of this effort is that the child has an increased chance for success. The child will benefit when parents and teachers engage in a positive, directive plan for the child where all parties demonstrate concern, respect for each other, and a willingness to work together.

The average classroom teacher today has had some information about attention disorder, but may not have been trained to manage it. Unless the teacher took a special workshop on the topic, she may or may not know how to design and accommodate the classroom environment to this child's needs. Many times parents have more information than the teacher based on their efforts to learn more about what they can do for their child. Some parents have done exhaustive searches and reading and have learned multiple strategies to help their child. These parents can be valuable team members if teachers appreciate the information they can share. When contributing information, parents need to remember to present it in a respectful and diplomatic way.

Using a Notebook

As a first step, parents should compile all the information they have received from private evaluations, school testing, etc. in a notebook. The notebook should also contain past test data, report cards, and other additional records. This notebook makes the entire collection of data and the child's immediate history accessible for any meeting should it be needed. Parents should take the notebook with them to every school meeting. It is invaluable when updating new and returning teachers on critical data and test documentation regarding the child. Parents who have shared the success of this notebook with me, often say that it saves critical time when the school team is unable to locate a document and they are able to produce it for the team.

Positive Parent Approach

Parents who are well thought of and accepted as an integral part of their child's educational team are those who are respectful, well-educated about their child's needs, and dedicated to the child's success. Parents who are unsuccessful in obtaining a smooth working relationship with the school are often demanding, rude, unprofessional, and impatient. The parent of a special needs child will want and need the school team's cooperation. To benefit from this collaboration, parents should introduce the most positive, well-intentioned, and well-informed presentation. Parents who come to a teacher meeting with notebook in hand and a list of their child's needs and strengths are far more likely to walk away with all the things they hoped for their child than the parent who is overbearing and uninformed about the laws and their own child's specific needs.

What Kind of Educational System is Best for the AD/HD Student?

Parents often ask me what the best educational environment for an AD/HD student is. They question a private school vs. a public school vs. home schooling. They ask, "Are smaller classes or larger classes more effective?" I tell these parents that the best choice is the school where they will be able to work closely with the teachers and staff and where they feel the staff is most responsive to their child's unique needs. In the **ideal** education model, we need to bring the environment to the child, and parents will want to choose the school team that is best able to do that.

From a practical sense, the public school should be the best prepared to serve the AD/HD child, since the laws relating to special needs children are part of the framework for public education. Tax dollars encourage support for the special needs child, and trained personnel within the public school system should be well-informed about both the individual disability laws and Section 504 of the Rehabilitation Act. These both play critical roles in the education plans of students with special needs. Private schools may offer smaller class sizes and a team that

will attempt to modify the curriculum to the student's needs. However, they may not be subject to the federal guidelines for handicapped children. Home schooling is a personal choice for a family and involves programming to provide the best curriculum on a one-to-one basis. I have children in my practice with AD/HD that have been and are successful at each one of these three educational choices. Overall, I find that the following points are key factors to consider in selecting the best educational situation for an AD/HD student.

Ideal School Environment

⚷ Responsive team that is knowledgeable about the disorder

⚷ Opportunity for smaller class size or smaller size experiences throughout the day

⚷ Diverse, integrated curriculum, flexible with variety yet structured with well-established routines

⚷ Parents respected and accepted as team members

What Kind of Teacher Will Be Most Successful with AD/HD Children?

The teacher with strong affective skills will be a highly successful teacher for the AD/HD child. *Affective skills* are skills that employ strong, visual-facial gestures and movement. Sometimes described as "the look," this skill is best illustrated by teachers whose facial expressions and manners quickly convey their messages. Teachers with strong affective skills are animated, direct, and use visual gestures to support their verbal directions. They are typically upbeat and convincing in their manner. Students immediately identify what they mean by their visual expression. There is no mixed message in the way they deal with students.

AD/HD children will probably have difficulty with a teacher who has low affect and gives mixed visual messages. They will no doubt struggle with a teacher who only uses verbal messages and appears stoic or unyielding. Their need for well-modeled visual directions will not be supported by a lecture format because they find it difficult to listen and focus on abstract concepts without visual or tactile support. Levine (1987) states that students with attention difficulties have areas of developmental dysfunction that impact their social abilities. The AD/HD child's inability to effectively read nonverbal feedback is one of these areas. Teachers can address this weakness in nonverbal association by using more visual cues than verbal, and by moving frequently within the room. They should model appropriate behaviors and also use students to role-model these behaviors. Daily schedules should include the opportunity for positive peer interactions and role-playing.

"I had a chance to observe the three third grade teachers at my daughter's school. Right away I knew Ms. Lopez would be a teacher Carly could relate to. She used great visual drawings, charts, and illustrations when she talked. She was easy to understand and gave brief, short directions. I saw her repeat information for some students in different ways, and she set up small class opportunities for children who didn't understand what she had presented in the whole group. She frequently had students act out what she was instructing and students served as direction helpers within the room. I put her name first on my list and justified why her style matched my daughter's needs." —Mother of a girl with AD/HD

Can a Parent Request a Teacher?

In some schools, parents are given the opportunity to request a teacher. In other schools, the team selects the teacher. Sometimes the school will permit parents to request a teacher in an end-of-the-year review of a 504 Plan or an Individual Education Plan (IEP). Parents of AD/HD children will want to let the administrator know which type of teacher their child seems to respond best to. Parents should be

aware that often the most popular teachers are those with good affective skills, and they need to be sure that the school personnel know they are trying to match their child's strengths to the teacher's and not just requesting a popular teacher. The parent who volunteers frequently at the school or has older children who have attended the same school will get to know the faculty and feel more confident about requests. Parents need to be very aware that there are some professionals who will not work well with the AD/HD child, and that they may need to move their child in the middle of the school year if the match between child and teacher is not a successful one. This change, although not always possible, may be the most effective solution for both parties.

Getting Under Way

Once the parents have met with the school team and have enrolled their child, they will be responsible for the child's preparation for school and his homework and study sessions outside of school. Parents should set up daily routines around the school day. It is helpful to start the day with an alarm clock to wake the reluctant AD/HD child and motivate him to get started. The sleep patterns of the AD/HD child are often irregular. He may take longer to wind down and fall asleep and thus be harder to wake up in the morning. Some researchers suggest that the AD/HD child is just getting into a deep sleep when it is time for him to get up! The AD/HD child may need more than the usual amount of rituals in the morning to get him up and going. Some parents tell me they need to use a series of alarm clocks to give their child multiple advance warnings before they enter his room. Many of my families tell me mornings are the most difficult time of the day for them. Figure 7-1 lists some suggestions to help parents prepare for this possible difficult time.

Figure 7-1: Morning Tips

- Have the child put out all of his school supplies the night before and set them by door. This includes his backpack, pencils, permission slips, assignment books, lunch, and homework.

- Determine which clothes he will wear to school and set them out the night before.

- Make a list of morning routines and place it on a white board in the child's room or in the bathroom. Have a dry-erase marker handy so the child can cross off each item as he accomplishes his morning tasks.

- Designate a specific time each morning to talk with your child about what his day will be like. Before he leaves for school, offer him key positive statements of reminders and cues.

Helping with Homework

For parents of children with attention deficit/hyperactivity disorder, homework time is often a difficult occasion when all participants experience frustration and disagreement. Due to their inattentiveness, these children will often exit school without all the critical information needed to even complete the homework as required. Parents often find themselves performing as tutors and organizational coaches. Here are some effective tips to help with homework routines.

- Establish a designated homework period.

- Keep all school materials in a brightly-colored plastic bag that hangs from the doorknob in the child's room. This way the materials are accessible and the parent can easily check to see if they need to be replenished.

- The homework area should be the same area every evening. Some AD/HD children do best with a consistent noise in the background to help them tune out other distracting noises. Many parents have found that a "noise box" or a "white sound box" is very effective. Some AD/HD children use earplugs to block out other noises in the home. Parents will need to determine which of these techniques is most successful for their child.

- Review the child's assignment notebook with him. Work with him to set a list of priorities, helping him plan what he will do first, second, and so on. Allow him to schedule time for personal choices other than homework so he will see that in a well-organized schedule, he can accomplish what he wants to do as well as what he has to do.

- It helps to place a mirror in front of some children while they do their homework. This way if they begin to daydream, they will catch their reflection in the mirror and they are more apt to get back on task (Goldstein and Zentall 2000).

- Timers (egg timers, numerical counters, etc.) are also helpful if used in a motivating, non–threatening way. Children can estimate how long they think the task will take and set the timer accordingly.

> *Positive example:*
> Parent says to child, "Set your timer to see how long it takes you to do your book report."
>
> *Negative example:*
> Parent says to child, "You have ten minutes to do this and if you are not done, there will be no television tonight."

Note:
If parents are unavailable when their child gets home from school, they may want to consider hiring a teenager as a "study buddy" who sets up a homework schedule and reviews assignments with their child. Local tutoring centers also provide study halls after school.

> *"The challenge before today's education professionals is to understand what an attention deficit disorder is, to understand normal development of attention, and to begin to set up strategies and interventions that allow this child to benefit from the educational environment."*
>
> —Clare B. Jones, Ph.D.

It is imperative for educators working with students with attention disorders to know what the disorder is and how it differs from other learning problems we see in the school environment. I believe the role of the teacher is literally that of an environmental engineer, one who arranges the learning environment for the child's success and who encourages learning through that environment (Jones 1994). In understanding the environment necessary to help AD/HD students succeed, the teacher needs to recognize that these children respond best to situations where they are asked to work in short brief chunks or segments, follow directions better when they are predictable and structured, and show a heightened interest when the teacher offers variety by changing routines and activities. Below is a brief description of the teacher's role and responsibilities as they pertain to the AD/HD student.

The Role of the Teacher of the AD/HD Child

1 Learn all you can about the disability.

2 Employ strategies, gimmicks, and interventions based on the child's needs.

3 Be proactive and positive.

4 Work with your teaching team.

5 Document your experiences—both successes and mistakes.

6 Stay in close communication with the child's family.

Production Deficit

Attention deficit is a production deficit. In other words, it is a performance disorder. AD/HD students are able to learn; they just do not produce or perform the work we expect. AD/HD students have great ideas and conversation about a task, but then they will not follow through with the completion of the task. A long-term assignment will evade AD/HD students; they prefer to get it over and get it done before they forget it. Parents report their AD/HD child will actually do homework and then forget to turn it in. For this reason, they must be taught memory techniques that trigger recall and follow through.

"They know what to do; they don't do it!" —Dr. Russell Barkley

Memory Techniques

Attention deficit children often experience difficulties with two types of memory—short-term memory and working memory. Therefore, it is critical for parents and professionals working with these children to introduce, teach, and model different memory strategies for the AD/HD student. Memory strategies include:

- *Mnemonic*—tricks or devices for remembering

- *Color-coding*

- *Oral and visual rehearsal*

- *Chunking*—breaking down what must be remembered into segments

- *Association*—linking things student already knows to material she needs to learn

- *Rhythm*—use of music, beat, chant, or patterns to engage in memory recall (e.g., poems, songs, and chants which recall a specific task to be memorized)

- *Chorale response*—stating information in "sound bites" or quotable clusters of words to make information more memorable

Parents and professionals often find the memory inefficiency experienced by the attention deficit child or student to be the most challenging feature of this disorder. Parents and professionals who work with this population often note they have experienced great frustration with this, even after intensive tutoring and modeling. For example, a parent might review and practice the memorization of a key element, such as math facts, with the child. The child will initially remember the information she practices, but the next day (often the day of a test) she cannot recall it when needed. This memory deficit is reported repeatedly about this disorder.

Attention deficit is the result of a non-performing activity in the brain that eliminates consistent and strong short-term memory. I advise my clients and audiences that it helps to keep this thought in mind, *"When you observe an inconsistent memory pattern time and time again, you must recognize that you are actually observing the disorder!"* Parents and professionals must recognize this memory lapse for what it is—a **disability** that will affect the child's follow-through and memory. Once you can accept this lack of consistent memory as the source of the disability, you are on the way to understanding the child's learning pattern. Then you can begin to devise and teach the child ways to cope with this lapse.

Brevity, Variety, & Structure

Students with attention deficits respond best to brevity, variety, and structure (Jones 1991). This means the child with attention disorders will be most responsive to activities that offer *brevity*—short, brief activities that allow them to stay focused and on task; *variety*—diverse activities that change the routine or heighten their interest; and *structure*—a routine or format that provides stability to the task. For example, the teacher should keep the classroom routines the same from day-to-day, but vary the tasks and teaching context within the routine. He might have reading at 9:00 a.m. each day, but some students might be reading with him, some might be working on the computer, and some might be at their desks doing word searches. The next day, the class may play a teacher-directed game, and, on the third day, the students might do a silent reading assignment.

If we can provide brevity, variety, and structure for AD/HD children within the learning environment, we can be more assured of meeting their specific learning needs. If, one day, they learn to add these three factors to their environment themselves, then they will have adapted and met their own needs. The professional who feels he is not maximizing the strengths of the attention deficit youngster will want to ask himself, "Did this activity provide brevity, variety, and structure? If not, how can I add those factors?"

 ### The Total Classroom Environment

Students with attention concerns are twice as likely to be distracted sitting in a classroom arranged in tables or desk clusters than they are in a traditional row arrangement. Due to their difficulties with social maturation and impulsivity, AD/HD students typically do not have the social skills or attention span to maintain focus in cooperative learning groups or group desk clusters. These seating arrangements make it more difficult for them to work independently. In research programs, students with AD/HD were increasingly distracted when placed in these cluster type arrangements. Professionals will want to work together to find the most successful seating arrangement for the child. Seating preference can be a personal accommodation, which is designated in a 504 Plan or Individual Educational Plan (IEP). The phrase "preferential seating," as designated in the federal guidelines for accommodations for attention deficit students within the classroom setting, mandates the teacher to help the student find the classroom seating arrangement which will best benefit her learning preference.

Teachers should avoid placing the attention deficit student near busy visual areas, activity centers, and the like. During large group activities, such as circle time and discussion time, it is most efficient to seat the children in a semicircle. Do not seat the child with AD/HD next to you; instead, seat her directly across from you where you can easily maintain eye contact. For floor activities, write the child's name on a piece of tape and place the tape on the rug. The child will look for her name, and it is easy to cue her to return to her "spot." This offers a structured approach to a random seating experience.

Figure 8-1 suggests some arrangements which work in favor of the AD/HD student's learning style. Hyperactive students usually do best when they are not distracting others around them. Therefore, they are often NOT successful in the front row of the classroom, as this area is probably the busiest and most distracting area in the room. They should be seated where they have a direct view of the teacher and an opportunity to stand and move when needed without bothering others.

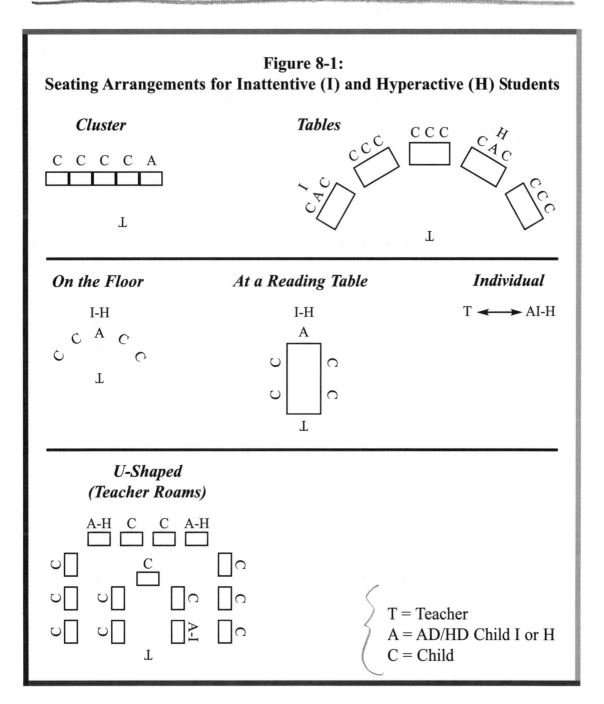

Figure 8-1:
Seating Arrangements for Inattentive (I) and Hyperactive (H) Students

The Organized Classroom

 Teachers will learn from trial and error that AD/HD students will be more productive and on-task in a classroom that is well-organized and managed. The classroom that has minimal distractions and offers quiet work areas with the use of headphones, when needed, is a start. The environment should show evidence of order and predictable scheduling. Tasks should be well-defined and directions for the tasks should be offered in both visual and auditory formats.

Students with attention concerns need advance warning before the transition to a new activity. They profit from well-defined transitions that provide ways for them to move from an unstructured activity to a slightly more structured activity to a very structured activity. For example:

go to recess

return to the room

have the class sing a song

discuss what will come next

have the class open their social studies books (structured activity)

Advance warnings of changes will prepare the students to anticipate the new direction in the plan, and they will generally respond more positively.

How to Offer Successful Transitions

1 Schedule time for the transition to occur. As you close one activity, review several interesting or motivating aspects of what is coming next (Jones 1998).

2 Offer cues that signal to the child a change is about to occur. Cues can include a song, significant words like "One, two, three, look at me," or visual signs such as a puppet or a colored card. ("When you see this colored card, what does it tell you to do?")

3 Provide step-by-step directions as to what will happen next. Hold up fingers as you state each step. ("Number 1, get your books out; number 2, turn to page 10; number 3, please look up when you are ready.")

Schedules

The AD/HD student benefits from a posted daily schedule where she can see that accomplished items have been crossed off, or more importantly, where she can cross off the items herself as she completes each activity. This routine offers a sense of security and order for the distracted student. Individual schedules are also helpful if she leaves the room for related services, such as speech or occupational therapy. When she leaves the classroom for such services, it is helpful to have a schedule posted in the room where she is going. This offers continuity in the day and helps build personal planning habits. All students in the class will react best to a visual, well-placed display of rules, schedules, and assignments.

Assignment Books

Daily plan books, which are often provided by the school for students, are very critical for AD/HD students. Initially, the AD/HD student may need more than one plan book since she will frequently misplace or lose hers. Help her color-code her plan book to make it easier for her to find subjects and information. For example, ask the student which color she associates with math. She can select the color that actually matches the book or a color she just feels matches the subject. If she feels the color red matches math, help her cover her math book in red. (There is a product called "Hot Covers" that is great for this. It is available at most stationary stores.) Next she should color-code her daily assignment book by drawing a red band across the page, indicating math. Then she should write her math assignment directly on this band. Use this color-coding system for each of the student's subjects. The student should use abbreviations, such as M for math, SS for social studies, and T for test throughout the assignment book. She can also use brightly-colored Post-it notes to mark specific pages and to help her find the months and days quickly.

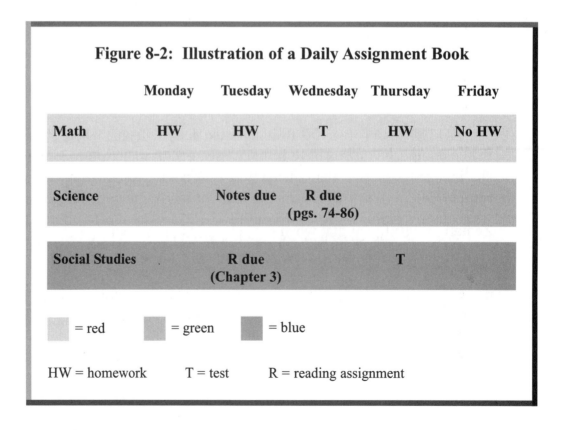

Figure 8-2: Illustration of a Daily Assignment Book

	Monday	Tuesday	Wednesday	Thursday	Friday
Math	HW	HW	T	HW	No HW
Science		Notes due	R due (pgs. 74-86)		
Social Studies		R due (Chapter 3)		T	

□ = red   □ = green   ■ = blue

HW = homework   T = test   R = reading assignment

If a student dislikes writing but excels at verbal discourse, she may benefit from taping her assignments rather than writing them down. She can use "minute minders," which are credit card-sized discs that contain up to three minutes of recording tape. She can tape her homework assignments and play back the verbal messages when she is at home and ready to start her homework.

Color Techniques

Color appears to play a highly specialized role in memory. Color-coding, in particular, appears as if it might be important for the rapid identification and recognition of objects. The use of color is well-documented as an integral part of many learning strategies. Several studies have concluded that improvement in recognition memory depended on the color comparison of presented images (Wichmann et al. 2002). Sydney Zentall, Ph.D. of Purdue University and Eric Jensen of The Brain Works in San Diego, CA, have written about the impact color has on the brain, memory, and people who have a challenge with memory. Zentall suggests color-coding materials for easy recall and even color-coding words, dates, and facts to engage the brain in more recall and comprehension. The purpose of these techniques is to produce an active memory pattern rather than a passive one. We know students with attention concerns remember the unique and the different, but often tune out the same, rote, and similar. Color-coding and color-recall strategies can help students recall clusters of material and retrieve minute details, which are often critical for follow-through skills.

Color can also be used to help with comprehension and recall. Sydney Zentall (1999) found that when students highlighted their reading materials in a specific color-coded pattern, they increased their comprehension of the material they were reading. She suggested that, when reading, students leave the first paragraph alone, highlight the entire second paragraph in one color, and highlight the third paragraph in a different color. She found that by repeating this pattern throughout the assignment, both students with attention deficits and those with learning disabilities had stronger recall of what they just read. If your students are unable to write in their school-purchased text, they may enjoy using colored highlighting tape. (See

Vendors of AD/HD-Related Products, pages 206-209 for ordering information.)

Group Work

The AD/HD child may struggle with classroom group work because she is often not focused enough to be alert and aware of others' participation. In brief, she is not a team player. Within the group, she needs more than the usual amount of structure, directions, plans, and suggestions for follow through. Because she often acts younger than her peers, group work may not be a successful strategy for her in school. Here are some strategies you can incorporate to help the AD/HD student when she is involved in group discussions.

Helping AD/HD Students in Group Activities

- Be sure each person in the group has a designated job.

- Post rules for each group on a colorful cue card and place it in the group as a visual reminder of the rules.

- Designate a time frame for the group activity and follow it. Announce when there are five minutes left in the time frame, so the members are aware of the transition and the termination of the work.

- Set up a system for taking turns in the group. For example, have a group leader use a checklist to be sure everyone participates once, or do an activity which insures each person's participation.

- Have a one-on-one review with the AD/HD child after the activity to be sure she understood your expectations and participated in the activity.

Individual Class Work

The AD/HD child is typically a poor self-starter. A teacher can help the AD/HD child manage individual work by creating a format or plan from which the child can begin to work. For example, let's assume an AD/HD child is having trouble starting on an individual worksheet assignment. The assignment is a math worksheet with 20 problems. The AD/HD student is looking around and fidgeting while the rest of the class is working independently on these problems at their desks. To support this inattentive student who needs a structured format to start her task, the teacher creates a plan. He goes to the student's desk and says to the student, "I will help you make a plan to get started on this task." The teacher then takes a colored pen and circles a small group of problems on the page. Then he puts a square around another group of problems and draws a triangle around a third group of problems. Finally, he draws a circle, a square, and a triangle at the top of the worksheet. The teacher then says to the student, "Here is your plan for this worksheet. Do the problems in the circle, the square, and the triangle. Cross off each shape at the top of your worksheet when you have completed it. When you have finished the problems in all the shapes, bring your paper to me." The student works the problems in each shape, crosses off each step of the plan as she finishes it, and takes the completed worksheet to the teacher. This plan is illustrated in Figure 8-3, page 112.

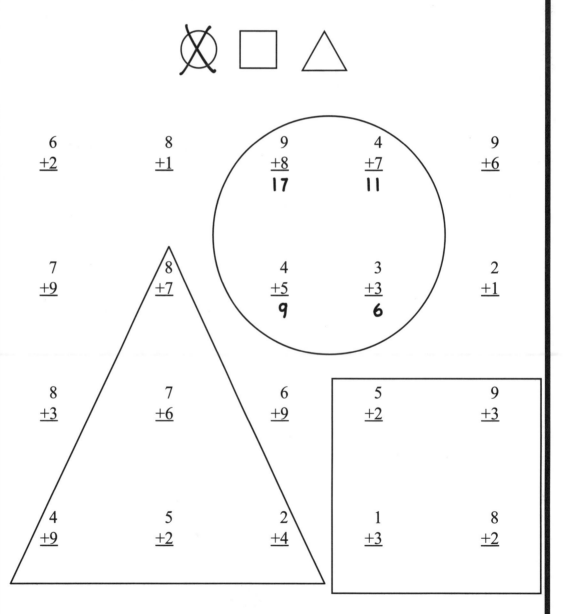

Figure 8-3: A Worksheet with a Plan

"Ashley, do the problems in the circle, then the square, and then the triangle. Cross off each shape on your plan when you have completed it. Bring your paper to me when you are done."

The teacher presented a visual organizer for the student that appealed to her need for brevity, variety, and structure on an otherwise boring worksheet. This strategy not only gave the student a definite plan to work from, it also created an incentive to complete each task. We cannot assume, however, that the child will automatically pick up this technique and manage it successfully the next day. To incorporate the variety the AD/HD child thrives on, the teacher will need to suggest another plan for her to model, such as, "You were so successful using the shape plan yesterday, let's try another plan today. Try to do all the problems on the math sheet that have an eight in them. Bring your paper to me when you have done that." This plan technique begins to guide the child toward setting her own goals and toward taking the initiative to start an assignment. The ultimate goal of this activity is for the student to be able to look at a worksheet and design her own plan.

Peer Tutoring

Peer tutoring is a technique where one student works with another student in the classroom to review and practice class work. It is a highly successful technique in many classrooms, but it is not as effective with AD/HD students because they are often more immature than their peers. Their poor social interaction skills put AD/HD students at risk in a peer tutoring experience with someone in their own class and age range. AD/HD students will do best when they can tutor younger students from a lower grade or when older students from a higher grade tutor them.

Individual Directions

Students with attention deficits may not be skilled in taking notes or writing assignments in their assignment books in an efficient manner. Their difficulties with visual-motor integration skills often make these tasks lengthy and time-consuming. Couple this behavior with their impulsive working style, and they may ignore critical directions on a worksheet and may miss key details they were to include. Here are some suggestions that will help AD/HD students learn to follow directions in a more efficient manner.

- Offer students highlighters so they can highlight directions on a page. This will help them slow down and review the directions.

- Have the students read the directions aloud to themselves and others.

- Make an overhead of a page from the class assignment book. At the end of the day, have a student helper write the homework assignments on the overhead sheet. Then the other students can copy them into their own books. Allow a different student to write on the overhead assignment sheet each day, so everyone in the class has an opportunity.

- Pair students together and have them check each other's assignment books. The recording of work in the assignment book at the end of the day will become part of the regular class routine.

Management

The daily schedule for children with AD/HD should incorporate an initial ritual activity that requires little planning. Because they are often slow starters, they may respond best to a more free-form activity during the first hour or class period. This activity should be followed by the bulk of the academic subjects in the morning. Since they tend to experience cognitive fatigue later in the day, AD/HD children will benefit from a highly-structured last period. The teacher should provide regular and frequent mental breaks but maintain structure in the time format.

Because of the AD/HD student's restless nature, she will need cues at the start and finish of an activity. Use "time-to-begin" cues and show definite endings to activities. When the student appears particularly restless, you may want to use a preplanned "secret signal" to allow her to stand or to remind her to try to maintain a little longer. This signal can be a tap to the side of your head, a wink, etc. This gives the child a visual cue that you understand her need for movement. Attention-getting devices can also serve to redirect the child and add interest and focus. Suggestions include playing a musical note, singing a musical stanza, and clapping or beating a pattern (when the children hear the clap, they join in with you). One effective technique is to use one green, one yellow, and one red transparency on the overhead. Put the green transparency on the overhead when students are working independently by themselves. Put on the yellow transparency when they need to settle down or lower their voices. And, when it is time to end the activity, place the red transparency on the overhead.

Note-Taking

Teachers can provide extended time for students who have difficulty copying notes within a class period. AD/HD students will benefit from the teacher adding numbers, marks, arrows, or boxes on the material they are trying to copy. This visual dimension adds a cue and a memory technique to enhance copying time, and may speed up this task for them. In addition, assigned student helpers can use carbonless notebook paper to provide copies of their notes for their fellow students who need this accommodation based on their significantly poorer writing skills. (See Vendors of AD/HD-Related Products, pages 206-209, for ordering information.) The additional copy of notes assures that the student who has poor note-taking skills will have a copy of well-taken notes to add to her own. Teachers can also help by giving students a copy of a note outline. Students can add to the outline, which features the main points of the lesson. One successful way to teach note-taking to AD/HD students is to use the web or mapping technique. This breaks the note-taking down into brief, manageable points and visually relates to the main idea.

Suggestions for Note-Taking

✓ Allow extra time for note-taking

✓ Add visual cues to material

✓ Use carbonless notebook paper

✓ Make up an outline with main points and let students fill in details

✓ Use web or mapping format

✓ Use a clipboard to hold paper and create a firm, structured surface

✓ Audiotape the lecture

Spelling Activities

The child with AD/HD often struggles with long-term recall of spelling patterns. As noted in Chapter 2, page 33, her pattern of "eclipsed" writing makes her spelling look irregular and careless. Suggestions to help the student with spelling are:

• Provide the student with a reduced list of spelling words compared to those given to classmates. Start with five words a week and gradually increase the list.

• Avoid using words the student does not know, use, or understand.

• Have the student type the words, write them in different colors, and spell them aloud on a tape recorder.

• Help the student study for spelling tests by providing a different homework activity each night to drill the words. Often, because AD/HD students are typically so skilled at immediate oral recall, they trick us into thinking they know the word. They can spell it right back, but they do not retain it. Therefore use a variety of different techniques.

• Encourage the student to create a word box of spelling words she has mastered or have her make a list of the words on her computer and add words to it as she masters them.

• Use separate grading scales to evaluate spelling tests. The AD/HD student can become easily discouraged when she constantly misses words on a test. Select point values based upon the number of correct letters rather than words (i.e., no correct letters = 0 points, one correct letter = 1 point, 2 correct letters = 2 points).

Tools for Success

There are a variety of supplemental tools that can be helpful to a student with attention difficulties. These physical tools are implements that may increase the student's efficiency within the classroom and allow her to feel more confident. They are useful materials that can enhance the student's learning.

Specific Paper

The AD/HD child will struggle with sequence, which makes the organization of ideas in a written format difficult. Simple adjustments in the paper selected for class work or note-taking can impact the written work of children with AD/HD. Pastel-colored notebook paper adds a focus or memory technique for rough drafts, writing assignments, and note taking. Students can use one color for each subject or use one color for drafts only. The color is easy on the eyes (less glare) and memorable in that like information is written on the same color. The paper also serves as a cue since it will stand out on the desk or work area, making specific papers easier to find.

Another type of paper that may be helpful for the AD/HD student is raised lined paper. This paper has a raised indentation at the bottom of each third line. These raised lines cue the student to stay on the line but also serve as a pressurized cue to keep writing. Some students respond well to this sensory input. As mentioned previously, the use of carbonless notebook paper for notes and other activities is also helpful. A student who is successful at the task can take notes on this paper, and then give the copy to an attention-challenged student. (See Vendors of AD/HD-Related Products, pages 206-209, for ordering information on these products.)

The AD/HD child needs to be able to see numbers in an orderly format, which can provide help with details in math. Graph paper (½ inch or one inch) is invaluable for keeping numbers in order or in columns. Its structured block format puts order and visual cueing into a math activity. Professionals should suggest that the AD/HD child use graph paper when she copies math work from the board to her paper and use it as practice paper when she is doing math worksheets. If graph paper is not available, students can use their regular three-ring notebook paper turned on its side with the holes at the top. This creates columns in which to write the numbers, thereby making it easier to keep the numbers in their correct positions.

Clipboard

The high activity level of many attention deficit students affects their physical management of the papers on their tables or desks. A simple clipboard to hold the wiggly paper can offer immediate structure and a feeling of order. Some students clip their pencils to their boards to prevent losing them. The clipboard is also easier to retrieve from an over-packed book bag.

Basic Notebook for Class

Parents should take their child to an office supply store and help her purchase the largest and best-built three-ring notebook available. It should have the following features:

- a large clamp for holding papers

- a clear pocket on the front. This is a very helpful spot for the child to display her class schedule. She can also decorate it by adding pictures or drawings.

- color-coded file dividers so student can identify subjects by name and color

- if possible, a small white marker board built into the cover of the notebook. Dry-erase markers are provided with this wipe-off board which can be very effective for quick notes.

In addition, you should purchase these items and place them in the front of the notebook.

- a three-ring zippered pouch to hold pencils and pens

- a plastic three-ring paper punch (now adapted to fit into a notebook) so student can punch papers her teacher passes back and place them directly into her notebook

- loose-leaf clear pocket pages to hold important papers that need to be seen immediately. (Students will want to avoid pocket folders since they frequently overload the pockets!)

Graphic Organizers for Webbing & Mapping

The technique of webbing, or mapping, is highly successful for many different learners today. The technique helps big picture thinkers to be more alert to details and helps them understand how material interrelates. Students can often link their notes more quickly to the content if it is presented in web or map format. Figure 8-4 shows an example of a graphic organizer used in teaching several characteristics about mammals.

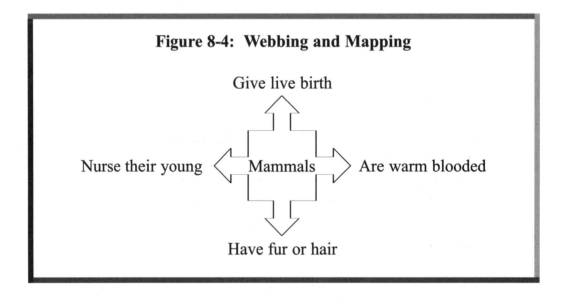

Figure 8-4: Webbing and Mapping

Give live birth

Nurse their young ⟨ Mammals ⟩ Are warm blooded

Have fur or hair

There are several software programs which promote webbing on the computer, but students can actively learn how to create their own webs on their notebook paper. One company, Learning Disabilities Resources (Center for Alternative Learning), publishes a packet of one hundred different graphic organizers for teachers to use as master copies. (See Vendors of AD/HD-Related Products, pages 206-209, for ordering information.)

Notes Home

It is important to keep the parents of the AD/HD child informed about their child's daily behavior and attention to task. Teachers can send home daily checklists or brief notes illustrating both positive and concerning behaviors that have occurred. Consistent communication with the parents of an AD/HD child will benefit the child's daily success.

Computer Software

There are multiple software programs that are highly successful with students based on their need for variety and brevity. AD/HD students are often drawn to the computer because their skills in multi-task activities respond to the structured, yet highly animated, visual information. Software programs can be helpful for the student with attention deficits and can be supportive strategies for them to employ throughout their lives. Here are some software programs I recommend to help the AD/HD student develop her skills in keyboarding, handwriting, webbing and mapping, writing, and studying. These products can be ordered from their individual publishers (phone numbers and/or web sites listed below) or from Cambridge Development Lab (CDL) by calling 1-800-637-0047 or logging on to their web site at *<www.edumatch.com>*.

- *Type to Learn Jr.* (grades K-2) and *Type to Learn* (grade 2 to adult). This software will help your child develop keyboard strategies and memory for the keyboard pattern. It offers brevity and variety in learning the keyboard. It is published by Sunburst and can be ordered by calling 1-800-321-7511.

- *Startwrite* is a software program that will help you create customized handwriting worksheets and lessons in both manuscript and cursive. You will be able to develop practice sheets that meet your child's individual needs. To order, call 1-801-936-7779 or log on to *<www.startwrite.com>*.

- Use the software *Inspiration* (K-College) to develop maps and webbing techniques for writing. It will help your child develop ideas and organize her thinking using webs or maps. To order, call 1-800-877-4292.

- The software *Expressions* helps a student go from brainstorming to a text outline format. It is especially rewarding for big picture thinkers who can generate ideas but not organize them when they write. It was created by Sunburst and is available at 1-800-321-7511.

- *Study Skills and Strategies: Special Needs*, published by Mangrum & Strichart, is a great piece of software to support learning study skills. It provides opportunities for active learning and student practice in study skills and strategies. The entire class can use this program, which comes with a reproducible activity book for the teacher. This product is available through CDL.

Computer Hardware

AlphaSmart is a handheld keyboard that is very sturdy and can be linked to a computer printer or main terminal. This handy keyboard can easily be placed in a book bag and carried into class. Using just a two-inch screen, it can record information from an outline or report. The student types in information and, later, when she plugs it into a computer, she will have a copy of the information she entered. *AlphaSmart* is less expensive than a laptop and almost indestructible. It provides a nice accommodation for the reluctant or disabled writer and is an appropriate first step to a desktop computer. It is available from AlphaSmart, Inc. and can be ordered by calling 1-888-274-0680 or logging on to *<www.alphasmart.com>*.

Gimmicks

Active, busy children seem to respond well to unusual gimmicks or tools. Figure 8-5 lists materials that are helpful for students with AD/HD.

Figure 8-5: Tricks of the Trade for Kids on the Go

☑ Post-it pads

☑ Post-it tape tabs

☑ Three-ring paper punch

☑ Carbonless notebook paper

☑ Large three-ring notebook

☑ Plastic bag that attaches to rings in notebook
   (for holding pencils and erasers)

☑ Colored dividers

☑ Colored note cards and colored note paper

☑ Clear plastic folders for important papers

☑ Mechanical pencil or gripper pencils
   (pencils with a pillow or grip)

☑ Handheld speller dictionary

☑ Assignment book or computer day timer

☑ Small tape recorder

☑ Computer (or AlphaSmart)

Working Within the Law: Understanding and Recognizing the Laws that Protect Children with Attention Deficits

There are federal regulations that have been developed to support children within a public school environment. Two of these regulations can be part of a service plan or therapeutic plan for a student with attention deficits. They are Public Law 101-476, the Individuals with Disabilities Education Act (called IDEA), and Section 504 of the Rehabilitation Act of 1973, a civil rights law prohibiting discrimination against persons with disabilities. These two federal laws provide that students with AD/HD must receive access to related services and/or special education when needed.

These two laws may require a multidisciplinary team evaluation of a child with attention concerns to determine what services are needed. A U.S. Department of Education Memorandum states that students with AD/HD are eligible for services based on the fact the disability is "a chronic or acute health problem resulting in limited alertness which adversely affects educational performance." In order for the child to receive services, the team must determine that AD/HD has a significant negative impact on her educational performance and classify her under the category "other health impaired" (OHI). If the child with AD/HD has another co-occurring disorder, such as a learning disability, a visual impairment, or significant language delay, she is also eligible for services if she meets the criteria for that disability. Once a school district determines that a child is qualified to receive services, the district identifies which program will best serve the child's needs. The school develops a written Individualized Educational Program (IEP) for each area in which the child is determined to be eligible to receive services.

Children who do not need special education may still be guaranteed access to related services under Section 504. The team may agree to develop an IEP for the child even if she does not qualify for services stating that they feel the services offered under IDEA best meet the unique needs of the child. A 504 plan is written for the child with attention concerns who does not necessarily have an additional documented learning concern but who will benefit from adaptations or accommodations in the classroom. This 504 plan, with its specific accommodations, is created with teacher, therapist, and parent input. The child can be involved in the process once she begins to realize more about her challenge and needs. Children typically sit in on these meetings when they are 12 or older.

What Does 504 Guarantee a Student with Attention Disorder?

This section of the law mandates that the school–aged child has a right to a free and appropriate education, including individually designed instruction. The 504 plan is a simple one to two page document which requires a statement regarding the nature of the school's concern and the basis for determining the disability. This written plan outlines how the disability has influenced the child's learning activity. The school multi-disciplinary team works with the parent and the child to develop a list of accommodations specific to the child's needs, and then documents that these adaptations will be met in the classroom. When completed, the plan is signed by all participants and placed in the child's cumulative file. The signed document is considered a legal contract between the child, parent, and school. Accountability must be demonstrated.

The school district makes the final determination regarding whether a 504 plan is necessary. If they decide to do an evaluation, they must send the parents a form requesting parental consent for the initial evaluation. The school does not need parental consent to implement the 504 plan, but they must notify parents of their right to contest the plan (Jones, L. 2002). If a family feels, for any reason, that the plan is not being implemented, or if they disagree with the school's determination or the types of services provided, they have the right to request a meeting to discuss the plan. If they are still not satisfied, they may appeal the decision and proceed to due process. Due process is a procedure, provided for by law within the public school, where the parties may debate and discuss the plan within a legal justice format. Attorneys for both sides are present and the decision is based on documentation of or lack of documentation of services.

The school is required to provide parents with information about appeal procedures. Should parents feel that their process had been denied they should check with the school, a local CHADD chapter, or a LDA (Learning Disability Association) chapter about their trained parent advocates. A local support group chapter or parent advocate service may be able to help locate a qualified attorney if one is needed.

What Are Typical Accommodations?

> *"Accommodations are provisions made in how a student accesses and demonstrates learning. These do not substantially change the instructional level, the content, or the performance criteria. The changes are made in order to provide a student equal access to learning and equal opportunity to demonstrate what is known."*
>
> —Arizona Department of Education 2002

Typical classroom accommodations include:

- Tailoring homework assignments

- Providing a structured learning environment

- Simplifying instructions about assignments

- Using behavioral management techniques

- Modifying test delivery

- Using compensatory tools such as tape recorders, calculators, and computers (aided instruction)

- Allowing additional time on written tests and assignments

- Giving preferential seating in room

- Giving advanced notice of tests and assignments

- Helping with assignment notebook or calendar

The accommodations are offered as need demands. Many children will develop their own adaptations and will master skills to serve their needs. It is important to consider which specific accommodations are needed at each grade level.

Typical Accommodations

Early Childhood

- Providing immediate reinforcement
- Clustering activities into short chunks
- Eliminating distracting elements in immediate play or work area
- Designing a structured class environment
- Implementing a behavior plan
- Giving preferential seating

Elementary School

- Giving advance notice of tests and assignments
- Helping with calendar or assignment book
- Giving preferential seating
- Implementing a behavior plan
- Extending time on written tests
- Giving support in copying from board to paper
- Modifying testing accommodations (e.g., taking the test in a quiet room, reading the test orally, using a ruler as cue for multiple choice format)

Middle School and High School

- Giving advance notice of tests or assignments
- Giving preferential seating
- Allowing preferential registration (matching classes and teachers to strengths)
- Modifying examinations including giving test orally, extending time, using enlarged text, allowing dictation of answers, altering the test format, and altering the language used including lowering the reading level
- Having someone else take notes or using carbonless note paper
- Supplying set of books for home and set of books for school
- Using auxiliary aids as needed (e.g., taped tests, computers, readers, interpreters, Braille readers, text enlargement devices, and alternative input devices)
- Allowing additional testing for college placement requirements
- Using books on tape or disc

Requesting the School to Do Testing

Parents of an AD/HD child who want to request the school to do further testing will need to put their concerns in writing and mail the letter to the school's principal, retaining a copy for their records. Figure 8-6 shows a sample letter to help parents contact the school in a professional manner.

Figure 8-6: Letter Requesting Evaluation

Dear Principal,

I am the parent of _____ who is a student in _____ (teacher's name) room, grade _____. My son/daughter was recently diagnosed with attention deficit/hyperactivity disorder by _____ (evaluator's name). For the past _____ years in school, his/her teachers have notified me of their concerns about his/her behavior and academic performance.

I am concerned about my child and have sought additional evaluation. I have this information from _____ (name of evaluator) and want to share it with the school. In addition, my child is not doing well in school and may require special education or related services. I am requesting a multi-disciplinary team evaluation to determine if _____ (child's name) is eligible for special education and/or related services under both IDEA (including the IDEA "Other Health Impaired" category) and section 504, in accordance with both state and federal guidelines. I hereby consent for this evaluation to be done.

I look forward to hearing from you in regards to this important manner. If I do not hear from you by _____, I will be calling your office directly. Thank you.

Sincerely,

_____

(Parts of this letter were adapted from the CHADD Guidelines under Educational Rights for Children)

A Master Teacher

Teachers and other related service professionals can best meet the needs of students when they attempt to offer services based on how successful they can be with accommodations. Teachers need to model a proactive attitude towards accommodations, not a punitive or negative one for procuring services. Once a student has the legal documentation stating she is to receive the services her disability merits, she should receive these benefits without sarcasm or feeling singled out. There is an art to offering the disabled person supportive services without making her feel like she is more dysfunctional in front of her peers. A teacher who handles adaptations in the curriculum well will do it with respect, honor, and an acceptance of what is fair. These teachers recognize all students are unique and that an important part of teaching is to instruct students so that they will eventually be able to advocate for themselves.

Fun Stuff Specifically Designed for AD/HD Students within the Class Environment

The following activities are designed to enhance the AD/HD student's classroom experience. They are a cluster of novel teaching strategies to augment any lesson.

Early Childhood

- Make a cardboard hand and staple it to a tongue depressor. Use it as a model for turn-taking. Point the hand toward the child when it is her turn to talk; point it toward you when it is your turn to talk.

- Teach patterning skills to young AD/HD children. Using a number of different items (e.g., paint sample chips, poker chips, magnetic shapes), make models of alternating patterns for them to imitate (e.g., blue chip, yellow chip, blue chip, and yellow chip).

- Place items children are working with on a cafeteria tray. This keeps items close at hand and separates each child's individual work activity from others at a table.

Elementary

- Use cardboard soda containers and Ziploc bags for loose desk items.

- After finishing a task, have the student name a suit from a deck of cards. Then turn over a card. If the suit matches the student's guess, she gets a one to five minute break.

- Tape a popular song each week and play it while students copy homework assignments from the board.

- Teach students to point to a sign (e.g., plus sign, multiplication sign) in math when they do it, or color it with a highlighting pen.

Middle School and High School

- Write three prompts of personal interest on a colored overhead. You might say, "Tell me your three favorite CDs, Tell me three places you want to go to someday, and Tell me three things you like about our school." These prompts will create an immediate activity for the students to do when they enter the room. After the students write their answers to the prompts, give them one minute to tell their partners or assigned buddies their answers. This activity can encourage transition skills and get the kids ready for the next activity.

- Try to greet each student at the door several times a week. This provides a strong visual and verbal contact immediately.

- Post the schedule and homework assignments on an overhead and leave it on throughout the class session.

- At the end of class, put a page from an assignment plan book on the overhead, and have a student in class volunteer to write the homework assignment on it. Then the other students in the class can write the information in their own assignment books.

For the Teacher

Every teacher has "trying times." Although behavior modification techniques and tips can be very effective, there are times when the following suggestions, using typical life examples, can be most helpful.

- *If your student shouts out in class*, use the response cost strategy described in Chapter 6 on pages 78-79. Use tokens or Post-its to remind the student that she loses an item every time the behavior occurs. Remind her that she can exchange any tokens she has left at the end of the period for predetermined privileges and rewards.

- *If your student fidgets, taps, or squirms in her seat*, offer short brief breaks when possible. Allow the student to hold appropriate items such as Wikki Stix. Be tolerant, ignore some of these behaviors, and move on!

- *If your student daydreams and seems to stare out in space*, gently cue her back on task with a soft touch or by moving directly into her area. To help prevent daydreaming, break up tasks by variety or color, and place the student's work on colorful paper or a place mat.

- *If your student forgets to return papers*, use boxes that are color-coded by subject to serve as appropriate reminders. Designate row captains to remind fellow classmates daily to turn in their papers and to inform you if someone needs an additional reminder.

- *If your student continually taps pencils on desk or books*, suggest "quiet tapping." Show her how to tap on her arm or pant leg instead of a noise-producing object.

- *If your student has difficulty following directions*, secure the student's attention before giving instructions. Accept that some AD/HD children will avoid your eye contact, but will still be listening. Limit your instructions to two or three steps. Hold up a finger for each direction you give. When you are finished, ask the

student, "What will you do next? Tell me the three things you need to do." Incorporate verbal gestures and visual reinforcement as you speak. Draw on the board or model the steps of process.

- *If your student needs to develop confidence and self-esteem*, praise her specific behaviors that you want to encourage. Say, "It is great to know you know how to do outlines. You underlined the key words just like we discussed."

Top Ten Tools for Teaching AD/HD Kids*

At the beginning of the school year in 2001, I was asked by *ADDitude Magazine* to write a "top ten" list for teachers working with AD/HD kids. I feel this list is an appropriate summary for this chapter as it reviews all the items we have discussed.

1 Avoid arranging the class in cluster or grouped desk arrangements. AD/HD children are twice as likely to be disruptive sitting in this arrangement. Try the U-Shaped or traditional model.

2 Send a regular communication log home. Let parents be aware of the child's behavior and progress in the classroom.

3 Color-code daily activities and materials that need to be remembered. Offer color cues as a memory device for forgetful students.

4 Employ devices to improve working memory. Offer mnemonics, music patterns, unique phrases, gimmicks, etc. to trigger recall and memory.

5 Offer a clipboard to active, busy writers. This gives the student a structured surface to write on and it keeps the paper stable, even in the hands of a lively child.

6 Teach list-making. Show children how to record priorities and then cross off tasks as they accomplish them.

7 Offer notebook paper in duplicate form. Carbonless notebook paper provides an immediate copy of notes. Ask the AD/HD child to take notes. Then, after class, supplement her notes with a copy provided by a more skilled note taker.

8 Offer Wikki Stix as an acceptable manipulative device when the child is required to sit and listen. These small plastic non-toxic strips give busy hands something to touch that won't be distracting to fellow classmates.

9 Structure transitions in your daily plan. AD/HD children have difficulty changing from one topic or area to another. Provide for this challenge by having definite transitions when you move from one topic to another. Transitions can include five, three, and two minute warnings; visual cues on the board for students to read; and songs announcing the next activity.

10 Take care of yourself! Take time to reward yourself. Remember to give yourself a pat on the back for the ideas and effort you are making for this child's success.

(* Jones, C. 2001. Reprinted with permission.)

> *"Coming together is a beginning; Keeping together is progress; Working together is success."*
>
> —Henry Ford

The team approach to managing an attention disorder will bring together individuals from several disciplines. Today's child with AD/HD often needs services that require him to interact with professionals who deliver multiple services. His individual needs will affect the membership of the professional team and, therefore, he may become involved with professionals within both the school and community environments. This multidisciplinary team benefits the child by sharing in decision-making, sharing their individual expertise, and providing new ideas for interventions. In all situations, the child's parents are essential members of this team. They will benefit from the multidisciplinary process because they will receive information from diverse professional perspectives.

Sometimes a parent will feel overwhelmed by the amount of professionals involved in these meetings and the information they have to share. They may feel more comfortable with an advocate present. An *advocate* is a person who understands the child's needs and, in addition, understands the laws pertaining to education. This advocate may be available through a local parent support group, the department of education, or a special needs center in your area. The advocate will accompany the parent to the meeting and act as a sounding board or personal advisor on the procedures at the meeting. To be prepared for a multidisciplinary meeting at school, parents need the following:

- notebook with paper and pens
- tape recorder, tapes, and batteries
- notebook containing any previous testing, school records, etc.
- any specific manual or booklet that is particular to their child's needs that they may want to refer to (e.g., a copy of the school transportation policy)
- list of prepared questions or concerns
- advocate, if needed
- positive, friendly, concerned demeanor

The multidisciplinary team may be comprised of administrative school personnel, specialists on specific learning concerns, the school nurse, parents, advocate, and any other invited guests. The team make-up will change depending on the situation and age of the child. The child should be part of the team once he is able to speak for himself and is ready to advocate for his own personal needs. I find the age when the child should start his involvement in the planning is usually around age twelve. Following are suggestions for the make-up of teams at several grade and age levels.

Suggested Participants for Multidisciplinary Teams

AD/HD Student's Preschool Team
- Psychologist
- Physician
- Nurse

- Parents and grandparents
- Preschool teacher/day-care provider/nanny
- Speech/language pathologist and other related services as needed

AD/HD Student's Elementary/Middle School Team
- Child (if twelve or older)
- Psychologist
- Physician
- Nurse
- Principal
- Tutors
- Special services as needed (speech/language pathologist, occupational therapist)

- Parents and grandparents
- Regular classroom teacher
- Social skills class instructors
- Athletic coaches
- Bus driver, if needed
- Nurse, if needed

AD/HD Student's High School Team
- Student
- Psychologist
- Nurse
- 504 coordinator
- Special services as needed

- Parents and grandparents
- Physician or psychiatrist
- Teachers
- Tutor
- Personal organization and strategy coaches

The Responsibility of Individual Team Members

The unique needs of an individual child will influence the membership of a multi-disciplinary team. Team members serving AD/HD children should be trained and knowledgeable in all aspects of the disorder. The value of a team or collaborative approach for the child with attention deficit is that it offers a well-defined reservoir of data on the child and provides interpretations from varied professional perspectives (Jones 1998). Parents are the critical nucleus of the team and their ultimate responsibility is to be the decision-maker for their child. Parents need to understand they are participating equally in this joint decision-making team, and that their choices will affect their child's growth and development.

Physician
When considering the needs of their child, the majority of parents will seek advice from the physician first. Not all physicians are aware of the guidelines for children with this disorder. Therefore, parents will need to ask the physician if he is up-to-date in this area and if he wishes to participate in the child's treatment plan. Because attention deficit is considered a chronic condition, The American Academy of Pediatrics Clinical Practice Guidelines recommends that physicians develop a treatment plan that is in collaboration with school personnel and parents. The guidelines suggest that school personnel should target management outcomes with the family's and the physician's involvement. The physician should provide a checklist for the parents to give to the teachers so periodic updates and communication can be achieved.

Nurse
The school nurse offers support to teachers and parents by providing the proper administration of medication. Nurses have been trained in observation skills and are a wonderful resource for schools when it comes to observing a student's behavior. They can facilitate the information-gathering phase by helping participants complete checklists and should be involved in the completion of checklists based on their own observations. During the period of time when a child is on a therapeutic trial of medication, the school nurse communicates with the physician and can gather before and after documentation of the child's

behavior. The nurse can provide a daily checklist of the child's medications: what he takes, the dosage he takes, and the time he takes them. These records are confidential for each student and the information is made available to the parents and physician only as needed.

Teacher

The majority of children with attention concerns will be in the regular classroom all day. It is critical for the regular classroom teacher to maintain behavior interventions and provide daily feedback and communication to parents. It is within the teacher's job description to develop on-going strategies for the AD/HD child. Some teachers are more effective at this than others. Some teachers seem to naturally adapt their environment to suit the child's learning style. These teachers are considered *master* teachers, and they are singly responsible for impacting and changing many children's lives.

Special Education Teacher

This specially-trained professional may be involved with the child with attention disorders if the child has a co-occurring disorder such as a learning disability. The special education teacher will offer specific learning techniques and strategies that are tailored to the student's individual learning style. She will write goals and objectives for the child to master within the time period they are involved in special instruction. This teacher may serve as an advocate and resource support person for the child in the mainstreamed teaching situation. She often administers specific achievement tests for evaluation and placement purposes.

Psychologist

The school psychologist is responsible for the majority of individual testing within the school district. The psychologist evaluates the child using a battery of tests and instruments that will enable parents and teachers to understand the child's potential and ability. Working with team members, the psychologist will offer suggestions and strategies based on the results of the test evaluations. He will observe the student in the

classroom setting and will often collect, review, and examine the behavioral checklists. The psychologist often chairs the multidisciplinary team of professionals who meet to discuss the child's IEP and/or 504 plan.

Speech-Language Pathologist

The speech-language pathologist (SLP) may play a large role in the success plan of a child with attention disorders. Many children with attention disorders experience difficulties with language and communicative control. The child study team within the school may refer the child to the SLP for evaluation. (Parents may also request in writing that an SLP evaluate their child.) The areas of concern in language that often are noted in the AD/HD population include difficulties with pragmatic language, listening skills, and semantics. The difficulties that are most noticeable in the AD/HD child include the following.

- He has a disorganized style of narrative that results in the listener sometimes saying, "What were we talking about?" The AD/HD child often fails to recognize the normal conversational cues in discourse. Other students and listeners will note that he fails to take in others' perspectives and seems egocentric as he talks.

- Listening skills evade him. Observers will note that he loses eye control and switches topics abruptly. He does not attend to relevant cues or stimuli.

- He is often unable to predict the consequences of his words and makes blunt, careless comments.

- His lack of selective and specific attention to details means he often walks away from a conversation with a wrong idea of what just took place. His impulsivity results in poor self-monitoring of his language and his blunt, forward, impulsive nature. It is hard for him to plan and self-direct because his short-term memory is so inefficient.

SLPs may be able to help this child if his performance on the language tasks indicates he qualifies for support. The SLP will introduce strong visual models to help teach the AD/HD child more adaptive social skills. Role-playing, acting out activities, and play-acting techniques will all be encouraged as supportive therapy. Some SLPs will employ the use of photographs which can be effective visual tools. The photos can depict appropriate social activities and interaction skills. The student is then asked to duplicate the behavior or attempt to model it. SLPs can also help in the modeling of turn-taking skills and staying on topic when communicating, which can help the AD/HD child practice his decision-making.

Occupational Therapist

The occupational therapist (OT) is trained to adapt the physical surroundings in school to facilitate the student's ability to function independently in that environment. Should a child with AD/HD demonstrate severe difficulties with fine-motor skills, conflicts with processing external stimuli, or poor motor coordination, the school may consult with an occupational therapist. The OT can be involved with an AD/HD child as a member of a multidisciplinary team. In this role, the OT can guide the team in understanding the difficulty the child has tuning out excessive stimuli in the classroom and sitting at a desk for a period of time. The OT may develop a variety of pre-writing activities to help the student develop a more fluid writing performance. Some of the ways an OT serves as a resource include:

- adapting and modifying the physical environment of the classroom to meet a child's needs.

- supporting activities that enhance visual motor integration. These activities include pre-writing activities, fine-motor tasks, visual tracing, or sensory motor integration activities.

- supporting handwriting skills. The OT may offer a gripper for a pencil when a child has a poor grip or suggest a slant board for writing to give the arm more support.

- developing a program that helps students, who have a more involved processing of stimuli difficulties, respond to high levels of stimulation in the classroom without losing control. These programs include tactile activities, deep-pressure techniques, and balancing. The OT may employ methods for relaxation such as playing soft music, using a white sound box, or using a large exercise ball as an alternative seating arrangement.

The use of sensory integration therapy as a support for students with AD/HD continues to be an area of research and study. Some OTs have suggested that students with this disorder may have abnormal vestibular functioning and that is what may make them hyperactive. At this point, "the assumption that students with attention deficit have abnormal vestibular function has not been proven" (Polatajko, H. et al. 1994).

For the Speech-Language Pathologist or Occupational Therapist

Every SLP or OT has "trying times." Although behavior modification techniques and tips can be very effective, there are times when the following suggestions, using typical life examples, can be most helpful.

- *If your client does not remember to come to your session regularly*, provide incentives and motivation for him to do so. Offer rituals that help key memory for returning. If a child is leaving a classroom to enter your area, provide a visual cue that hangs in the classroom on that specific day as a reminder or place it directly on the child's desk when he enters the room.

- *If your client becomes silly and acts like a class clown in your session*, ignore his behavior. Look to children who are modeling positively. Redirect their attention to you by making the class activity more interesting. Make what you are doing so enticing that the other children will ignore the clown. Use verbal cues to emphasize how interesting the task is. This verbal engagement can redirect the AD/HD child's attention to your activity and away from entertaining others.

- *If your client becomes distracted in conversation and talks incessantly*, employ good eye contact. Ask the child specific details regarding what he is talking about. Question who, what, why, where, when, and how. Ask these types of questions to guide the child to become more specific with his line of conversation.

- *If your client has difficulty taking turns in a small group session*, select an item for each child to hold when it is his turn, such as a paper microphone or a nametag that says "My Turn." All participants look at and listen to the person who is holding the microphone. If a child interrupts, your eyes should remain on the speaker, thus visually cueing the child who interrupted that "all eyes are on the speaker."

Successful Intervention with a Multidisciplinary Team

The success of children with attention deficit within the school can often be attributed to the hardworking team members who have established and supported the child's need for accommodations. Many of today's AD/HD students are doing well thanks to the dedication of school teams and the development of appropriate and adaptive school curriculum. These teams have learned that when the 504 plan works, everyone benefits. A list of key steps to successful intervention with the team is on the next page.

Keys to Successful Intervention with a Multidisciplinary Team

✍ Work closely with the parents to provide a united effort and approach.

✍ Follow the guidelines for providing well-integrated, developmentally-appropriate instruction and activities.

✍ Be aware of the signs of difficulty and provide adequate stimulation and intervention.

✍ Avoid attaching stereotypic labels to particular behaviors.

✍ Be responsive to each child's individual needs and abilities.

> *AD/HD affects the lives of millions of women, yet few receive the comprehensive treatment needed to alleviate the impact of its symptoms and to optimize functioning.*
>
> —Patricia O. Quinn, M.D.

Out in Space with Stephanie

Stephanie appeared to everyone around her as the perfect eight year old—quiet, cherubic, and blue-eyed. Friends and relatives all labeled her the "all-American good kid." Perceptions changed, however, when Stephanie entered second grade. That's when both parents and teachers began commenting more on Stephanie's inability to focus and her daydreamer style than on her other attributes. Stephanie's mother was very concerned and suspected everything from physical illness to early signs of puberty, but she was completely surprised when a school psychologist suggested the possibility of AD/HD. She had only a mild understanding of attention disorder and thought that it was typically an area of concern for hyperactive, out-of-control boys. When the psychologist began describing the characteristics of inattentive symptoms, Stephanie's mother said, "That describes my daughter perfectly, but I think it also describes me!" She promptly scheduled an appointment for herself and her daughter with a well-respected clinical psychologist. The school psychologist's perception and Stephanie's mother's insight proved to be accurate. They were both diagnosed with attention deficit inattentive type!

Stephanie began on a treatment program that emphasized strategies for school, focus, and medication. She began to keep up with her peers, and both she and her mom became active in mother-daughter therapy sessions. Within six months, both mother and daughter demonstrated the benefits and success of their multi-modality treatment plans. Stephanie and her mother joined the recent ranks of young women being diagnosed with a disorder that for years was considered only a male disorder. Of every ten children referred for possible AD/HD diagnosis and treatment, only ONE is a girl. Research in the past four years estimates that at least one in three children with AD/HD will be female. At the adult level, the statistics for referral and diagnosis are one adult male to every adult female.

Why Aren't Girls Referred as Often for Attention Deficit?

The first and most frequently-noted reason for a lack of referrals is that girls often seem to experience attention disorders without the more obvious hyperactive features. The boy with attention disorders is apt to have the very visible symptoms of activity and poor impulse control. AD/HD tends to manifest itself in most girls in an almost silent manner, with symptoms like inattentiveness, daydreaming, and forgetfulness. This lack of overt physical movement or "hyper" behavior makes the disorder less obvious to the observer. For example, the "typical" AD/HD boy might respond to his teacher's reprimand about a lost paper by saying loudly, "So what! Who cares?" The AD/HD girl in the same situation may just sit in her seat daydreaming and not respond to the teacher at all. She might be thinking, "Why didn't I return that paper? I must be dumb!" In fact, many girls with the disorder begin to internalize their feelings and develop lower self-esteem and personal anxiety as they question their own inattentive ability. The result of this perceived difference is that a girl is more apt to be ignored for her inattentive behavior, whereas a boy is more apt to get an immediate response from the teacher who notes his behavior.

The second reason why girls have not been referred as often or their symptoms have not been studied in depth has been the lack of women in medical research over the years. In most medical research models, the male has been the dominant choice of study. The emphasis on women's disorders has been largely neglected in the past due to gender bias within the medical and scientific communities. As more women join the ranks of medical researchers and as educated women speak out and seek information, we are beginning to see a new direction and a focus on medical research with an emphasis on female samples.

What Other Factors Can Impact Girls with Attention Disorders?

Recent research by a team at Harvard University, headed by Dr. Joseph Biederman, found that 45% of AD/HD girls have a co-occurring disorder. This co-occurring disorder is usually clinical depression or anxiety disorder. This additional symptom begins to influence the girl's actions and her performance in schoolwork

and on tests. When tested intellectually, girls with AD/HD score lower on intellectual and academic achievement instruments than other girls their age. Researchers suggest that this is not due to lower cognitive functioning, but that it is caused because these girls are more anxious and possibly depressed. Therefore, they perform more poorly on the actual tests than their cognitive skills warrant.

The fact that they are internalizing their fears and exhibiting anxiety, thus reducing their self-esteem, places the girls at a higher risk when coping with society. They become more likely to experiment with drugs and alcohol and are at a greater risk for teen pregnancy. Once these girls are diagnosed, they begin to understand what the challenge has been in their lives. Then many of these young women depict the anguish of their struggle to be "quiet, in-control, and organized" (the expected behaviors society has deemed necessary for teen-age females). Their inability to conform often makes them critical of themselves and others, and they experience shame for not being able to play the role society expects them to play.

It is also interesting to note that some young women experience more difficulty with the disorder when they reach 18 and leave the formal structured atmosphere of the home. Once they lose this support system, they find they are unable to cope with this lack of structure and routine in their lives.

When Are Most Girls Diagnosed?

Girls are often diagnosed later in life than boys are. Today most boys are diagnosed in kindergarten or first grade. But, because the onset of symptoms appears to be later for girls, many of them are not referred until puberty (around middle school). Also, the symptoms girls experience seem to get more severe as they age, while boys seem to experience some relief from their symptoms as they get older. Adult psychiatric clinics report a much higher percentage of AD/HD women than men coming in for support.

Puberty is generally accompanied by mood swings and over-reactivity. Girls, in particular, experience increased mood fluctuations when they are under hormonal influence. The AD/HD girl going through puberty will experience these symptoms in a more intense manner. Thus, "coming of age" tends to interrupt the cognitive

function with hormonal dysfunction. As a result, the AD/HD girl does not have the coping strategies to easily get through this time in her life. New research in hormonal deficiency in girls with AD/HD is a focus in medical investigations. The results continue to bring beneficial information to females.

So What Do We Look For?

When evaluating behaviors and symptoms in the female suspected of AD/HD, the following characteristics need to be considered.

Girls with inattentive attention deficit will typically:

- appear passive or introverted in class.
- daydream and may appear shy or timid.
- forget to bring papers and other items home.
- have trouble following multi-step directions .
- begin to show signs of low self-esteem ("I can't do this." "I am so dumb!").
- find their minds wandering when they read.
- lose track of time and will frequently be late.
- have a messy book bag, car, purse, and room.
- be forgetful in daily activities.
- give up quickly and be easily overwhelmed.
- make careless errors.
- remember something one day, but not the next.
- differ in their socialization with other girls.
- fidget, twirl their hair, or pick their cuticles.

Academically, girls with attention disorders will:

- be inconsistent in their academic performances.
- score lower on standardized instruments than expected.
- have difficulty with reading comprehension.
- have difficulty with written language skills.
- experience difficulty with sequential tasks.
- not volunteer in class.

A minority of girls diagnosed will exhibit the classic symptoms of hyperactivity. They may be hyper-talkative and reactive. They may adopt behaviors such as excessive talking and/or impulsive behavior and may get nicknames like "Chatty Cathy" or "Tomboy Terry." They are often teased or ridiculed for these overt behaviors because these behaviors are typically viewed as "boy-like characteristics" and are not well-accepted in females. A girl can also be diagnosed with the combined category of AD/HD, that is, she may show symptoms of both hyperactivity and inattentive behavior.

What Can You Do If You Recognize These Symptoms in a Girl You Know?

If the girl is twelve or older, ask her to read some passages and materials about attention disorder to see if she can relate to the examples. (See Resources for Females on pages 202-203 for a list of books, periodicals, and web site addresses.) Once the girl has read the information, ask her, "Can you relate to any of the things you read?" or "Do the behaviors described seem anything like what you feel during a day?" If the girl is under twelve, give the reading material to her parents to read, and then ask for their interpretation of the material as it relates to their daughter. If the girl or the adult states that the experiences she has just read about seem typical, ask the parent to complete the checklist in Figure 10-1, page 150.

Figure 10-1: Does Your Daughter, Friend, or Student Have AD/HD?

Read this checklist to the girl and write in her *yes* or *no* response to each item.

_____ I have trouble finishing my assignments in class.

_____ I daydream in class.

_____ Even when I try to listen, my thoughts wander.

_____ I forget to bring my papers and permission slips home from school.

_____ I have trouble following the teacher's directions.

_____ My mind wanders when I read.

_____ Projects and papers are hard for me to finish.

_____ I often do my work at the last minute and turn things in late.

_____ I get upset more easily than my friends.

_____ Sometimes it feels like I'm not good at anything.

_____ I am frequently late.

_____ It is hard for me to concentrate when there are people around me.

_____ My parents and teachers tell me I do not try hard enough.

_____ Other kids tease me about being spacey.

_____ I feel different from other girls.

_____ I lose track of time.

_____ I have a messy book bag.

_____ My room at home is a disaster.

Note: This checklist is courtesy of *ADDvance Magazine* <*www.addvance.com*>, a publication for women and girls with AD/HD.

Count up the "yes" responses. If the child gave an affirmative answer to at least half (9) of the questions, further testing is recommended. If her "yes" responses are significant (more than half), it is time to arrange an evaluation by a professional who is experienced at diagnosing AD/HD in women and girls.

Once You Have the Diagnosis, What Do You Do?

As soon as a family has received the diagnosis of AD/HD for their daughter, they will want to consider several critical areas. The following lists for the parent and for the teacher or therapist will serve as resources.

For the Parent:

☺ Let your daughter understand your unconditional love, and make sure that the statement comes across loudly and clearly.

☺ Help your daughter understand that this is a hidden disability and one that people will not easily recognize. Explain how you were convinced that she had this disorder and what steps you took to learn more about it.

☺ Encourage your daughter to read information or listen to tapes about AD/HD. Use a common sense definition and explanation of the brain, such as the one described by authors Kathleen Nadeau, Ellen B. Littman, and Patricia Quinn in their book *Understanding Girls with AD/HD*. Make the diagnosis real for her.

☺ Talk about what *will* and *can* happen, NOT about what *won't* and *can't* happen.

☺ Teach your daughter to use "Self-Talk." This is positive verbal language to guide her through difficult times. There is no room for doubt or negative comments, such as "I am just stupid." She should replace comments from her past with positive, affirming statements like "I can do my best," "I will try to do all I am asked," and "I have tricks to help me remember what I need."

☺ Make cue cards or stickers of positive quotes, such as "Just do it," "Yes I can," and "I will!" and place them in important places for your daughter to see.

☺ Find true-life, success stories of similar girls to use as inspirational guideposts. (See Resources for Females, pages 202-203.)

☺ Begin to collect a toolbox of gimmicks to help your daughter organize her materials and manage her time. Collect colored stickers, Post-it notes, calendars, a calculator, and colored highlighters. Make sure these tools of organization are readily available at all times.

☺ Look for a study skills class or an organizational workshop in your area that your daughter can attend. Make it a special reward, not a punishment. Perhaps you could pay the tuition for a close friend of hers to also attend or plan a special lunch after each session. It should be a fun experience that she will look forward to and value. Look into SuperCamp (see page 160) as an alternative to learning these skills in the summer.

☺ Celebrate differences! Revel in the unique style of learning that you have now discovered is HER way of learning. Vow to work with her to continue to keep her spirits alive and well.

☺ Make a list of all the great things she does and post it in a place where you can both see it and add to it daily.

☺ Keep learning! Stay in tune with the field through the Internet and be alert to the new information in this fast-growing field.

For the Teacher or Therapist:

☺ Take time to read the report provided for you by the parents. If possible, talk to the professional who made the diagnosis.

☺ Ask if the disorder is mild, moderate, or severe. Review the information from Chapter 1 of this book to help you understand the different levels and what to expect.

☺ Determine what accommodations you may offer to support the girl in the classroom. As you read earlier in this book, accommodations vary and need to fit the student's individual needs.

☺ Avoid referring to the AD/HD diagnosis as the girl's *problem* or *difficulty*. Use positive, affirming language that incorporates words such as differences not disabilities, strengths not just weakness.

☺ Offer a brief time each day when the girl knows she can approach you for advice or support. Make it a structured time you both respect and use.

☺ Present academic tools that offer brevity and variety. To help the inattentive student stay involved, encourage highlighting notes and making interactive notes.

☺ Teach webbing and mapping as an effective note-taking strategy.

☺ Stop periodically in your lectures for review and visual cueing of important facts and data that must be reviewed.

☺ Encourage using the computer and using compensatory strategies like the tape recorder and electronic day organizers.

☺ Set up "buddy check points" throughout the day. Announce that pre-assigned partners or buddies will look at each other's notes to see if they are on track and check each other's assignment notebooks to see if assignments and test dates are recorded properly. Encourage all classmates to cue one another for important details. This maintains a working team environment for all students.

☺ Be an active team member. Send home brief notes to the girl's parents to keep them up to date on her progress. **Notify them immediately when you see a change in behavior or performance.**

☺ Never lose sight of the positive model you can be in this girl's life. Reward the positive behaviors you see and encourage the strengths by pointing out what she does well.

Additional Gimmicks for Girls!

Here are some additional strategies that will be helpful to both parents and professionals working with girls with AD/HD.

- Research indicates teachers often fail to call on girls with inattentive attention disorders because they tend to "fade into the woodwork." To make sure you call on all of your students equally, write all their names on tongue depressors. Then put the tongue depressors in a tin can on your desk. When it is time to call on someone, choose a stick. This gives every student an equal chance.

- In addition, help the inattentive, possibly anxious child by stating, "This question is for David, but the next one will be for Stephanie." This alerts your inattentive student to be ready. Privately let the student know you will always give her a warning before she is requested to respond.

- Assign students to cooperative learning groups by carefully reviewing class strengths and weaknesses. Balance your groups so one person is not always dominant. Switch group roles often. Understand that most AD/HD children will need you to help assign them to a group, as they may not feel accepted.

- Assign responsibilities. Often a teacher avoids the AD/HD student when she looks for someone to do special jobs in the class. Make it a point to include these students in class responsibilities. If you feel a student cannot do an entire job for you, break the job up into sections. For example, say, "Craig and Lindsay, please divide these papers and hand them back to your classmates for me."

- Provide colored note cards. These cards are used to hide or minimize distracting information and allow the student to focus on one item at a time. Use colored pens and chalk on the board to emphasize key points. Have extra markers available for anyone to use.

- Encourage the use of color-coding and other mnemonic memory tricks. Make it "cool" in your class to share memory strategies.

- Remember to break tasks into short, brief segments whenever possible.

- When you give directions make sure they are clear and concise. Offer directions in both a visual and verbal format. Make a written copy of your oral directions and give a copy of it to each student who needs to read it to learn.

- De-stress the entire class before a test. Review what will be on the test, highlight excellent ways to study for the test, and have an in-class session to model what your students should do at home to study for the test. Prior to giving the test, allow everyone a minute to sit quietly and take three deep breaths. Then pass out a plain white sheet of paper to everyone. Say, "I know there are some things you have been hoping you would not forget when you take the test today. Use this paper to write them down now, so they will be there for you when the question comes up." This strategy often eases the tension for test takers. It can create a healthy atmosphere for test taking.

- Every Friday, take five minutes and have your students write down five things that were important in their lives that week. Call it your "Fab-5" (*Fabulous Five*) minutes. Each student jots down five things they learned, did well, or liked about the week. (Everyone deserves time to reflect and evaluate her skills.) As your students "take five" to review their own notes, share five positive things you observed about your whole class.

> *"The good sides of AD/HD far outweigh the bad. Think of it — we have boundless energy. If you want somebody who will constantly think of new ideas, we're it!"*
>
> —Keith Brantly, 2001

What factors contribute to make a person with attention deficit disorder successful? Is it a strong understanding of his disability and how to advocate for himself? Is it the fact that he lives in a home where his parents are concerned, organized, and determined that their child will succeed? Is it the fact that he had a team of educational professionals who recognized his unique needs and learned to accommodate them? Finally, is his success based on the correct pharmacological treatment plan? I believe that all of these factors play a part in the life of a person with attention concerns. As he grows older, the chances are great that he will experience success in his lifetime if these factors are an integral part of his life.

Resources for AD/HD Children and Their Families

There are a variety of resources that AD/HD children and their families can use to guide them through the complex phases of this disorder. Here are some things families and caregivers will want to consider along the way.

Coaching

The job of coaching is a profession that has grown in response to the needs of the person with attention disorders. Using the spirit of what the word *coach* embodies, these professionals help their clients by listening, supporting, and guiding them to make important decisions in their lives.

The idea of a person coaching another through an activity was first referred to in the book *Driven to Distraction*, in which the authors, Hallowell and Ratey, described coaches as helpful in offering encouragement and direction for a person. They described a coach as "an individual standing on the sidelines with a whistle around his neck barking out encouragement, directions, and reminders to the player in the game." They suggested that people with attention disorders might respond to a coach.

Professionals involved in coaching today are from a variety of backgrounds (therapists to retired teachers), but despite their diverse history their goals are common. Coaches will listen to the AD/HD person and help him set goals for himself. They will then help him devise a plan for achieving those goals. They will cheer the person on as he strives for success, and finally, they will help him evaluate his efforts. For more information about coaches check out these resources:

- American Coaching Association
  1-610-825-8572
  www.americoach.org

- ADD Coach Academy
  1-518-482-3458
  www.addca.com

- OFI-Optimal Functioning Institute
  1-865-524-9549
  www.addcoach.com

Parents As Coaches

Parents may want to try the role of coach also. Parent coaches will help their children develop and practice the skills necessary to cope with the attention deficit. Dr. Steven Richfield has written a book to help parents learn to adapt ways to coach their children. This unique parenting technique is featured in his book *The Parent Coach*, published by Sopris West.

■ Sopris West
1-303-651-2829
www.sopriswest.com

Tutoring

Most school-age students with AD/HD will need a tutor sometime during their years in an academic environment. Their challenges with focus during sustained work times make them prime candidates for missing critical information during the day. They often need tutors not to TEACH them the subject but rather to show them how to review the subject, how to study the subject, and how to organize their material for class.

During the child's elementary years, parents provide the tutoring help. But, as the child grows older, parents begin to find that tutoring their emerging adolescent is too stressful and discover it is a job best handled by an outside professional. Most students with AD/HD will obtain a tutor during middle school or high school, and it works to their advantage. It releases the parents from feeling like nags and, ultimately, makes for a better parent-child relationship. In addition, the child slowly becomes less dependent on his parents. The dependency transfers to the tutor, and eventually, the child becomes independent.

Tutors of children with AD/HD should have the following goals:

- Provide an orderly, well-planned period with a schedule and an agenda openly displayed.

- Incorporate organizational techniques and teach personal strategies of follow-through and maintenance.

- Contact teachers and be aware of long-term assignments and schedules.

- Set up plans, guidelines, and incentives for homework but do not do the homework for the student.

- Model good organizational skills, such as planning and management of materials.

- Teach the student color-coding techniques.

- Maintain good communication with the parents and the student.

- Have all materials organized and available.

- Keep the work area or table uncluttered. Display only the materials needed.

Summer Activities

The summer is a great time to help the child with AD/HD build self-esteem and develop skills and talents that he did not have time for during the year. Look for camps that have diverse activities and also teach team building and goal-setting skills. Here are some well-known resources that offer summer programs for AD/HD children.

■ **SuperCamp**
  1-800-385-3276
  www.supercamp.com

This motivational study skill-based camp, which runs weekly throughout the summer, is generally located on a college campus somewhere in the West. Past locations have included Stanford, Claremont College, and the University of Colorado. The techniques enhance personal self-esteem, organization, and study habits.

■ **Landmark College and High School Summer School**
1-802-387-6718
www.landmark.edu

This campus, located in Putney, VT, is exclusively for students with learning disabilities and AD/HD. They have an accredited summer school program for high school and college students. They employ strategies and interventions and have a low faculty-student ratio.

■ **Camp Buckskin**
1-218-365-2121
www.campbuckskin.com

This wilderness camp located in Ely, MN specializes in serving youth with AD/HD. They use outdoor activities, camping, and boating as a way to help campers produce changes in attitude and develop coping skills.

■ **SOAR**
1-828-456-3435
www.soarnc.org

This is described as a wilderness adventure program that provides opportunities for AD/HD children from age 8 to 18. The SOAR camps emphasize support in life skills, organization, and social skills. Courses are in over eight different states, Belize, Canada, and Costa Rica.

Books on Tape

For many years students who are blind or have a learning disability have had the opportunity to benefit from the audio presentation of a book or text. These books on tape have made a significant difference in these students' ability to successfully interpret printed material. Books on tape now include CD formats and have expanded the role of the computer as an additional tool. Students with attention concerns may also qualify for these services if

they have a co-occurring reading disability or reading comprehension difficulty. If their attention deficit reduces their performance significantly when reading independently and they benefit from audio interpretation, they will want to pursue this service. Books on tape/disk/CD are available at a minimum charge to qualified students. Services are available through the following associations:

- Recording for the Blind & Dyslexic
  1-609-452-0606
  www.rfbd.org

- Braille Institute Library Services
  1-800-272-4553
  www.braillelibrary.org

- Clearinghouse for Specialized Media and Technology
  1-916-319-0791
  www.cde.ca.gov

Scanner System

About 25% of the students with AD/HD have a co-occurring learning disability. If they have difficulty with reading speed and comprehension, one exciting tool to enhance their reading support is the Kurzweil 3000 System which links the book they are reading to a computer and scanner. This system scans any printed material, displays a full-color version, and then reads the book aloud. The student can read along, take notes, and highlight words right on the computer. A built-in talking dictionary allows the student to look up a definition immediately. The system includes a printer and a collection of tools that support study methodologies.

- Kurzweil 3000 System
  Kurzweil Educational Systems, Inc.
  1-800-894-5374
  www.kurzweiledu.com

The Student Day-Timer

This planner goes beyond the normal assignment book and offers an entire system of color-coded calendars, class schedule sheets, project planning forms, grade tracking sheets, study sheets, and study tips. There is a notepad, file pockets, and a security pocket.

■ Day-Timers, Inc.
 1-800-805-2615
 www.daytimer.com

The Watch Minder

This digital watch includes a beeper and a voice message system to help with personal organization and time.

■ 1-800-961-0023
 www.watchminder.com

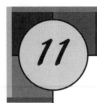

Success Stories: Ready...Set...Win!

The following exciting stories are adapted from actual clients' cases. These are typical clients that I have worked with in my practice in Scottsdale, AZ. They are just a few of the incredible people those of us who work in the field of attention disorders meet every day. I wanted to share their personal victories with you.

Jenny is best described as overactive, impulsive, and hurried. A psychiatrist diagnosed her at age 17 after a dismal senior year. She had been receiving mediocre grades and had inconsistent test scores on standardized tests most of her life. Her parents wanted her to move forward with the diagnosis, work with a counselor on goal-setting, and obtain a personal coach. Jenny decided not to take any of the recommendations because she felt she would "grow out of it" in college. She stated she wasn't sure she even believed the diagnosis. She went to junior college and dropped out with failing grades at the end of the first semester. She was unable to keep up with the demands of the college environment, both academically and socially.

What Worked?

Jenny came to my practice and we rewrote her goals. First, I suggested that she move from a major that was detail-oriented to one that offered a more concept-based, action-oriented career (business accounting to education). I encouraged her to move from a semester school to a quarter school and recommended that she begin to tape her lecture classes, buy summaries of texts when available, and work with a tutor on study skills and organizational techniques. Together we drew up a daily personal goal list, and I encouraged her to participate in study groups. I felt that she needed to be involved in regular physical activity and suggested that she try aerobics. Finally, I encouraged her to try extended-release medication. Jenny started back to school taking the minimum number of hours and working immediately with the special services department at the community college.

Winner!

Jenny will graduate this year with her teaching degree in early childhood. After two and a half years, she transferred from the community college to a four-year university. She is a part-time teacher at the college aerobics center, and she is considering teaching in an inner-city school.

Mike, a young boy whose parents were both physicians, was severe AD/HD and very bright. One of his personal interests was raising rare birds, and he was also a gifted musician who played by ear. Mike was hard to get out of bed in the morning and stayed up very late at night. He was continually missing classes. He constantly complained that his classes were boring; however, he never completed any assignments even in classes of high interest. He remembered things that were unique and different, but could not remember to put his name on a paper. He eventually dropped out of high school at age 16. He had developed some oppositional behavior and was becoming a chronic debater. His parents were paralyzed, unable to believe their child was so unsuccessful at school.

What Worked?

I encouraged Mike to take the GED and he passed the first time. I arranged for him to start working with an AD/HD coach three times a week. He and the coach connected in many ways, and it was this coach who encouraged him to take a job in a music store where his strength as a musician would be recognized. The store manager understood Mike's difficulty with organization and details and allowed him to work more with customers than financial details. Mike now attends community college. The coach suggested that Mike arrange his class schedule so that he has late morning and afternoon classes only. I suggested that he start with a small class load, selecting his first classes by interest not requirement. I made this suggestion to engage his need for high interest first. Then, when he has established some success, he can move on to the more traditional first year classes.

Winner!

Mike's relationship with his coach has made a big difference. He chose not to use medication at this time. He has regular strategy sessions for memory and follow through with his AD/HD coach, and he also works on his academics with a tutor. He appears to be doing well and enjoys his job and classes. He has stated that his goal is to become a veterinarian.

Mario, a personable young boy, had great difficulties in kindergarten and first grade. Teachers were engaged by his friendliness and brightness but were concerned with his hyperactivity and lack of self-control. They were very concerned that it would interfere with his learning. A variety of behavior strategies were implemented at school, including a response cost program where Mario had to be accountable for his outbursts. After Mario's mother, a single parent, met with the teachers at school, she began to read more about disabilities that may affect behavior. She noted many of Mario's behaviors as being consistent with his father's difficulties. She talked to Mario's paternal grandmother who described her son (Mario's father) as impulsive and inattentive as a child. Mario's mother asked the teachers if they felt Mario's problems might be attention related. They suggested she seek an evaluation by a school psychologist and that she talk to Mario's family doctor.

What Worked?

Following further evaluation, Mario was diagnosed with attention deficit disorder. Mario benefited from both "pills and skills." His mother read everything she could about attention disorders and became knowledgeable about how the school could help, the laws affecting her son, and how he could best be his own advocate. She was actively involved in his treatment plan and worked closely with his physician and teachers. Mario was on extended-release medication throughout high school. He experienced no side effects. He was active in student government and volunteered at the Boy and Girls Club throughout his high school years, and he became an Eagle Scout. Mario had a 504 plan put into place his eighth-grade year after a difficult time with follow through and homework. During his sophomore year he began working with an organizational tutor and put his daily schedule and planner on his laptop. In his senior year, he applied for and received accommodations (extended time qualifications) on the SAT and ACT. Mario was accepted at all three of his colleges of choice. In the letter he wrote for all his applications he spoke openly about his attention concerns and what he has done to cope with them. He chose to go to the state university, which he felt had the best record for supporting AD/HD students. He recognized he had benefited from the study tools and accommodations he has had and wanted to avail himself of services on the college campus.

Winner!

Mario is now attending the university where the unique programming options are tailored to his type of learning. He actively participated in the interview with the school special services department and works closely with the personnel there. He uses a tutor to help with the organizational demands of his life and classes. He benefits from student services and accommodations provided by the department on campus for students with disabilities. He will graduate in two years and is considering graduate school.

*W*elcome to the Attention Deficit/ Hyperactivity Disorders Workshop! This section is designed for the professional who will be presenting materials to staff members in a workshop or in-service presentation. The following pages can be reproduced in overhead format or scanned for a PowerPoint presentation. If you have read this book carefully, you will be able to use the key information included on these pages to help your audience understand this disorder in a complete and factual way. Pages 17-19 of this workshop can be used as a handout for your audience. Please be sure you share that this is copyrighted information. I hope the workshop will be helpful for your staff.

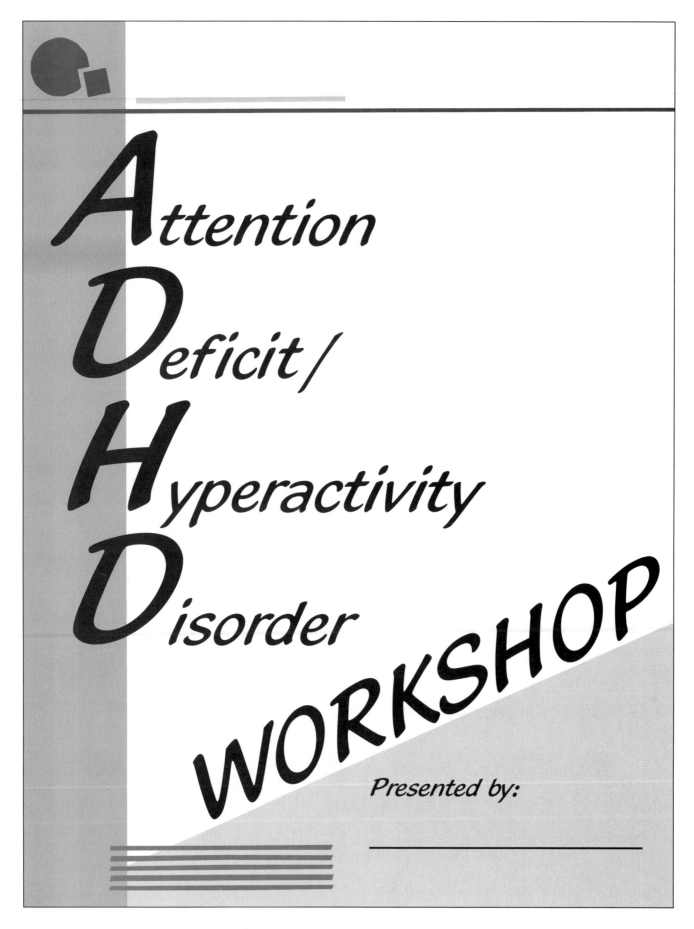

Attention Deficit/ Hyperactivity Disorder

WORKSHOP

Presented by:

_____

Workshops Work!
Practical Suggestions for AD/HD
Author: Clare B. Jones, Ph.D.

Disclaimer:

The materials used in this workshop are compiled from *Practical Suggestions for AD/HD* authored by Clare B. Jones, Ph.D. and published by LinguiSystems, Inc., East Moline, IL.

These materials are copyrighted. Any reproduction or distribution of these materials, other than for use with this workshop, is prohibited.

Workshops Work! 1
Practical Suggestions for AD/HD
Author: Clare B. Jones, Ph.D.

Copyright © 2003
LinguiSystems, Inc.
1-800-776-4332

Diagnostic Statistical Manual

- Attention deficit-primarily inattentive type, exhibiting six or more of the recognized symptoms

- Attention deficit-primarily hyperactive impulsive type, exhibiting six or more of the recognized symptoms

- Attention deficit combined type

- Attention deficit not other specified

To make the diagnosis, we need . . .

✓ Family History

✓ Developmental Signs

✓ Physical Observation

✓ Interaction

✓ Parent and School Checklists

✓ Psychoeducational Battery—
allows us to see strengths and
weaknesses of student and if student
is eligible for accommodations under
504 or IDEA

New Research

1   Chromosome studies yield definite pattern

2   FMRI imaging notes unique brain imprint

3   Studies of dopamine indicate irregular levels in hyperactive persons

4   Girls have same diagnosis but respond differently

5   AD/HD can be mild, moderate, or severe

6   70% have mom or dad who also has it

What works?

- ○ Educational interventions

- ○ Behavioral modification strategies

- ○ Parents understanding of disorder and self-examination

- ○ Developing healthy self esteem

- ○ Medication interventions

- ○ Fostering social skills

Practical Suggestions for AD/HD
Author: Clare B. Jones, Ph.D.

What doesn't work?

- Ø Herbal therapy

- Ø Biofeedback

- Ø Megavitamin therapy

- Ø Diet restricting sugar and food dye

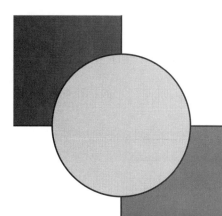

Federal Provisions

- Eligible for accommodations within classroom if failing to learn—Section 504

- May be eligible for IEP under other health impaired if team agrees

- Eligible for accommodations in school, testing, higher education, and workplace.

Co-Morbidity

Medical term for two or more disorders ——————
occurring at same time ——————

- Learning Disability in up to 33% of AD/HD

- 50% may meet criteria for disruptive behavior disorders

- 25% of AD/HD have anxiety and 10% to 30% have mood disorders

- AD/HD occurring in 25% to 75% of tic disorders

Practical Suggestions for AD/HD
Author: Clare B. Jones, Ph.D.

Copyright © 2003
LinguiSystems, Inc.
1-800-776-4332

Profile of an AD/HD Child

Strengths:

- verbal
- big picture thinkers
- often creative
- strong visual gestalt skills
- ideas
- long-term memory

Weaknesses:

- organization
- visual details of rote or similar nature
- poor recall of sequence
- short-term memory
- impulsive

Practical Suggestions for AD/HD
Author: Clare B. Jones, Ph.D.

Three Key Words

1 *Brevity*: activities of short duration

2 *Variety*: diversity, change in pattern or routine

3 *Structure*: routine, order, form

Practical Suggestions for AD/HD
Author: Clare B. Jones, Ph.D.

Educational Interventions

- ✔ Accommodations

- ✔ Assignment books

- ✔ Breaking tasks into chunks

- ✔ Checklists

- ✔ Color

- ✔ Extended time

- ✔ Graphic organizers

- ✔ List-making

- ✔ Mnemonics

- ✔ Offer transitions

- ✔ Opportunity to hold
  or manipulate materials

- ✔ Organizational tools

- ✔ Preferential seating

- ✔ Sending notes home

- ✔ Unique rehearsal

Practical Suggestions for AD/HD
Author: Clare B. Jones, Ph.D.

Tools for Success

✗ Books on tape or disc

✗ Carbonless notebook paper

✗ Clipboard

✗ Color highlight tape

✗ Colored note cards

✗ Computer

✗ Mechanical pencil

✗ Second set of books

✗ Rap tapes of facts and other information

Behavior Interventions

- Finding out what student does well

- Providing structure and routine with brevity and variety

- Token programs for children under age 8

- Daily note home to parents

- Menu of reinforcers

- Redirection

- Short, brief instructions with eye contact

- Response cost

Social Interventions

AD/HD students perform better in independent sports (martial arts, swimming, golf, biking, etc.).

Encourage early involvement with multi-age groups

Position in sports makes a difference

By middle school, these students need a mentor, coach, or tutor

Encourage participation in activity that offers routine and discipline

Practical Suggestions for AD/HD
Author: Clare B. Jones, Ph.D.

What Lies Ahead?

- Eligible to take SAT, ACT, and graduate school tests with accommodations

- Eligible for extended time testing

- Eligible for programs at university under special services/unique offerings

- Accommodations available into workplace if employer notified (ADA)

Practical Suggestions for AD/HD
Author: Clare B. Jones, Ph.D.

Resources

Jones, Clare B. (2003).
Practical Suggestions for AD/HD. East Moline, IL:
LinguiSystems, Inc.
1-800-776-4332
www.linguisystems.com

Richard, G. and Russell J. (2001).
The Source for ADD/ADHD. East Moline, IL:
LinguiSystems, Inc.
1-800-776-4332
www.linguisystems.com

CHADD National Support Group
(Children and Adults with Attention-Deficit Disorders)
1-800-233-4050
www.chadd.org

Course of Action

Once the diagnosis is given, parents begin the following course of action:

1 Understand the disorder. Learn what it is and what it is not.

2 Introduce bibliotherapy to the child: A selection of books is available for children on the subject of attention disorders. Parents can select several of these books and begin to help their children understand their challenges through stories that describe how other children have succeeded.

3 Attend parenting classes, participate in support groups, and obtain reading material.

4 Obtain resources: Information is available at local libraries, in bookstores, on the Internet, and through support groups.

Steps to Follow

Depending on what age level the child is at, the following steps are helpful for families.

Lower Elementary Grades (First through Third Grade)

→ Inform and involve the teacher: Parents guide the teacher to understand the child's needs and strengths.

→ Encourage the child's personal growth through the selection of outside school activities.

→ Confer with a physician on the pros and cons of the use of medication.

→ If medication is selected, inform the school and monitor its daily use.

Upper Elementary Grades (Fourth through Sixth Grade)

→ This is a critical time to teach the child study skills and personal organization skills.

→ Introduce strategies for school success. Teach self-advocacy and know how the child learns best.

→ Support and guide the child in social skills. Help the child adapt to peer groups and to develop team skills and appropriate socialization skills.

Middle School

→ Reinforce and gradually encourage independent skills.

→ Teach responsibility.

→ Develop a 504 plan if needed. The student should be involved with the team in designing the plan.

→ Help the student find or join a group or activity that will provide a regular social link to other students, yet offer the discipline, order, and responsibility this child needs. Suggestions include band, chess club, photography club, drama club, athletic team, etc.

High School

→ Work with a counselor to select teachers and classes that match the student's academic talents and interests.

→ Provide tutoring for any subjects in which the student is unable to keep up with daily demand.

Workshops Work! 18
Practical Suggestions for AD/HD
Author: Clare B. Jones, Ph.D.

Copyright © 2003
LinguiSystems, Inc.
1-800-776-4332

→ Have the student take preparation classes for the college admission tests - SAT and ACT.

→ Allow the student to take driver's education with obtaining a license as a goal. Many AD/HD students and their families put this milestone off a year or two until the student's maturation level is more appropriate for this responsibility.

→ Decide on the type of higher education or vocational pursuit.

→ Involve the student with a part-time job based on his individual strengths.

→ Guide the student in sexual planning.

College and Beyond

→ Understand the American Disabilities Act (ADA) and how it may affect a job in the future.

→ Find a college that offers accommodations for the AD/HD student.

→ Encourage the student to attend marriage and family planning sessions.

→ Learn about graduate school accommodations.

→ Learn about workplace accommodations.

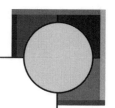

Achenbach, T. M. & Edelbrock, C. S. (1986). *Child behavior checklist and revised child behavior profile.* Burlington: Department of Psychiatry, University of Vermont.

American Academy of Child and Adolescent Psychiatry. (1991). Guidelines for the diagnosis of attention deficit hyperactivity disorder. *Journal of the American Academy of Child and Adolescent Psychiatry*, 36, 138-157.

American Academy of Pediatrics. (2001, October). Clinical practice guideline: Treatment of the school-aged child with attention–deficit/hyperactivity disorder. *Pediatrics*, 108, 4.

American Medical Association. (2001, October). *Pediatrics*, 108 (4), 1033-1044.

American Psychiatric Association. (1987). *Diagnostic and statistical manual of mental disorders-third edition.* Washington, D.C.

American Psychiatric Association. (2000). *Diagnostic and statistical manual of mental disorders-fourth edition.* Washington, D.C.

Arizona Department of Education Web Site. (2002, February). *Definition of Accommodations. www.ade.state.az/us/ess/ACCOMfin.asp.*

Barkley, R. (1991). *Hyperactive children: A handbook for diagnosis and treatment.* New York: Guilford Press.

Barkley, R. (1994). What to look for in a school for a child with ADHD. *The ADHD Report*, 2, 1-3.

Barkley, R. (1998, May). The effects of methylphenidate on the interactions of preschool ADHD children with their mothers. *Journal of American Academy of Child and Adolescent Psychiatry*, 27 (3), 336-341.

Barkley, R., & Mash, E. (Eds.). (1996). *Child psychopathology.* New York: Guilford Press.

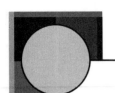

Beery, K., & Buktenica, N. A. (1989). *The developmental test of visual motor integration (Beery VMI) – revised.* Cleveland, OH: Modern Curriculum Press.

Biederman, J., Milberger, S., & Faraone, S. V. (1995). Impact of adversity on functioning and co-morbidity in children with attention-deficit hyperactivity disorder. *Journal of the American Academy of Child and Adolescent Psychiatry*, 29, 698-701.

Bossard, J. H. S. (1992). From *The best of success: A treasury of success ideas.* Compiled by Wynn Davis. Lombard, IL: Successories Publishing.

Brantly, K. (2001, October). Always on the run. *ADDitude Magazine*, 8, 8-9.

Brooks, R., & Goldstein, S. (2001). *Raising resilient children.* Chicago, IL: Contemporary Books.

Brown, T. (1999). In *Parent articles about ADHD* (page 10). San Antonio, TX: Communication Skill Builders.

Brown, T. (Ed.). (2000). *Attention–deficit disorders and co-morbidities in children, adolescents, and adults.* Washington, D.C.: American Psychiatric Press, Inc.

Carlson, C. L., Pelham, W. E., Milich, R., & Hoza, B. (1993). ADHD boys' performance and attributions following success and failure: Drug effects and individual differences. *Cognitive Therapy and Research*, 17, 269-287.

Castelhanos, F. X. (1997). Approaching a scientific understanding of what happens in the brain in ADHD. *Attention!*, 41, 30-35.

CHADD. (1998). *Facts #4-Educational rights for children with ADD. www.chadd.org.*

CHADD. (1999). *Fact sheet on AD/HD.* Landover, MD: CHADD Headquarters.

Clarke, A. R., Barry, R. J., McCarthy, R., & Selikowitz, M. (2001, November). EEG-defined subtypes of children with attention-deficit/hyperactivity disorder. *Clinical Neurophysiology*, 112(11), 2098-2105.

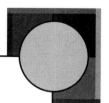

Cooley, M. (2002, June). The medication dilemma. *Attention!*, 6, 34-37.

Covey, S. (1990). *The seven habits of highly effective people.* New York: Simon & Schuster.

Dendy, C. (1995). *Teenagers with ADD: A parents' guide.* Bethesda, MD: Woodbine House.

Flint, L. (2001). Challenges of identifying and serving gifted children with AD/HD. *Teaching Exceptional Children*, 33, 62-69.

Goldman, L. S., Genel, M., Bezman, R. J., & Slantez, P. J. (1998). Diagnosis and treatment of attention-deficit/hyperactivity disorder in children and adolescents. *Journal of the American Medical Association*, 279, 1100-1107.

Goldstein, S., (1999). In *Parent articles about AD/HD* (page 5). San Antonio, TX: Communication Skill Builders.

Goldstein, S., & Jones, C. (1998). *Managing attention disorders (revised).* New York: John Wiley and Sons.

Goldstein, S., & Zentall, S. (2000). *7 steps to homework success.* Plantation, FL: Specialty Press.

Guevara, J., Lozano, P., Wickizer, T., Mell, L. & Gephart, H. (2002). Psychotropic medication use in a population of children who have attention deficit/hyperactivity disorder. *Journal of Pediatrics*, 109, 733-739.

Jensen, E. (1998). *Teaching with the brain in mind.* Alexandria, VA: Association for Supervision and Curriculum Development.

Jones, C. (1991). *Sourcebook for children with attention deficit disorder.* Tuscon, AZ: Communication Skill Builders.

Jones, C. (1994). *Attention deficit disorder: Strategies for school age students.* San Antonio, TX: Communication Skill Builders.

Jones, C. (1998). *Sourcebook for children with attention deficit disorder.* San Antonio, TX: Communication Skill Builders.

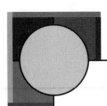

Jones, C. (2001). Why Johnny can read. *ADDitude*, 9/10, 18-20.

Jones, C. (2002). *The source for brain-based learning.* East Moline, IL: LinguiSystems. Inc.

Jones, C., Searight, H. R., & Urban, M. A. (1999). In *Parent articles about ADHD* (47-48). San Antonio, TX: Communication Skill Builders.

Jones, L. E. (2002, February). *General overview of 504* (paper presented to Arizona Law conference). Scottsdale, AZ.

Korn, M. L. (2001, October). *Information for clinicians: AD/HD.* American Psychiatric Association - 53rd Institute on Psychiatric Services.

Lavoie, R. (2002, Spring). Self esteem: The cause and effect of success for the child with learning differences. *Schwab Learning Newsletter*, 1.

Levine, M. (1987). *Developmental variation and learning disorders.* Cambridge, MA: Educators Publishing Service, Inc.

Levine, M. (1993). *All kinds of minds: A young student's book about learning abilities and learning disorders.* Cambridge, MA: Educators Publishing Service, Inc.

Levine, M. (1994). *Educational care.* Cambridge, MA: Educators Publishing Service, Inc.

Levine, M. (1997). *The ANSER system: Aggregate neurobehavioral student health and education review (revised).* Cambridge, MA: Educators Publishing Service, Inc.

Levine, M., & Jordan, N. (1987). Learning disorders: The neurodevelopmental underpinnings. *Contemporary Pediatrics*, 4, 16-43.

Nadeau, K., & Quinn, P. (Eds.). (2002). *Understanding women with AD/HD.* Silver Spring, MD: Advantage Books.

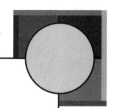

Pelham, W. E., Murphy, D. A., Vannata, K., Milich, R., Licht, B. G., Gnagy, E. M., Greenslade, K. E., Greener, A. R., & Vodde-Hamilton, M. (1992). Methylphenidate and attributions in boys with attention-deficit hyperactivity disorder. *Journal of Consulting and Clinical Psychology*, 60, 282-292.

Pharmaceutical Research and Manufacturers of America. (2002). *The 2002 survey of new medicines in development for children*. Washington, D.C.

Phelan, T. W. (1998). *1-2-3-Magic: Training your children to do what you want!* Glen Ellyn, IL: Child Management, Inc.

Polatajko, H., Law, M., Miller, J., Schaffer. R., & Macnab, J. (1994). The effect of a sensory integration program on academic achievement, motor performances and self-esteem in children identified as learning disabled: Results of a clinical trial. *Occupational Journal of Research,* ii, 155-176.

Rapoport, J. (1995). *New findings in brain development in children with ADHD*. Washington, D.C.: Seventh Annual Conference, Children and Adults with Attention Deficit Disorder (CHADD).

Roberts, B. (1998). *Phoebe flower's adventures*. Bethesda, MD: Advantage Books.

Ross, D. M., & Ross, S. A. (1982). *Hyperactivity-current issues, research and theory (2nd edition)*. New York: Wiley and Sons.

Schatz, A. M., Tallantyne, A. O., & Trauner, D. A. (2001, December). Sensitivity and specificity of a computerized test of attention in the diagnosis of attention-deficit/hyperactivity disorder. *Pub Med*, 8(4), 357-365.

Snyder, M. (2001). *AD/HD and driving*. Whitefish, MT: Whitefish Consultants.

Solanto, M. (2002). The predominantly inattentive type of ADHD. *Attention!*, 8, 6.

Swanson, J. (1999). Combining methylphenidate and clonidine. *Journal of the American Academy of Child and Adolescent Psychiatry*, 38, 620-622.

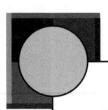

References

Talan, J. (2002, October). Attention-deficit disorder/ADHD children found to have smaller brain size than peers. *Newsday*, A18.

Teeter, P. A. (1998). *Interventions for ADHD*. New York: Guilford Press.

Utah Public Mental Health System. (2002, July). *Utah public mental health preferred practice guidelines*. Salt Lake City, UT: Utah Public Mental Health Committee Publication.

Wechsler, D. (1991). *Wechsler intelligence scale for children - 3rd edition (WISC-III)*. San Antonio, TX: The Psychological Corporation.

Weiss, G., & Heichman. L. (1986). *Hyperactive children grown up*. New York: Guilford Press.

Wichmann, F., Sharpe, L., & Gegenfurtner, K. (2002). The contributions of color to recognition memory for natural scenes. *Journal of Experimental Psychology*, 28, 3, 509-520.

Zentall, S. S. (1995). Modifying tasks and environments. In *Understanding and managing children's classroom behavior*, edited by S. Goldstein. New York: John Wiley.

Zentall, S. S. (1999). Working toward homework success for the adolescent. In *Parent articles about ADHD* edited by Jones, Searight, & Urban, 147-149. San Antonio, TX: Communication Skill Builders.

Zentall, S. S., & Kruczek, T. (1988). The attraction of colors for active attention-problem children. *Exceptional Children*, 54, 4, 357-362.

Ziffer, R. (1990). Who wants to play with Jason? *Play!*, 1, 1, 10-12.

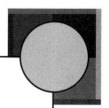

Camps

■ **Camp Buckskin**

Summer Address	Winter Address
P.O. Box 389	8700 W. 36th St., Suite 6W
Ely, MN 55731	St. Louis Park, MN 55426
1-218-365-2121	1-952-930-3544
www.campbuckskin.com	*www.campbuckskin.com*

- An overnight summer camp program for students ages 6-18
- Located at Camp Buckskin in Ely, MN.
- Techniques emphasize self-esteem, social skills, organizational skills, and coping skills

■ **Landmark College and High School Summer School**
River Road South
Putney, VT 05346
1-802-387-6718
www.landmark.edu

- A summer school program for high school and college students
- Located at Landmark College in Putney, VT
- Offers skill development courses in writing, reading, communication, and study skills to develop self-management, self-understanding, and self-advocacy

■ **SOAR**
P.O. Box 388
Balsam, NC 28707-0388
1-828-456-3435
www.soarnc.org

- A wilderness adventure program for students ages 8-18
- Located throughout Southeast, Florida Keys, Caribbean, Rockies, and Desert Southwest
- Techniques emphasize life skills, organization, and social skills

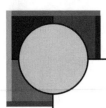

Resources

- **SuperCamp**
  1725 South Coast Highway
  Oceanside, CA 92054-5319
  1-800-285-3276
  www.supercamp.com

  - An academic summer camp for students ages 9–24
  - Generally located on a college campus somewhere in the West
  - Techniques enhance personal self-esteem, organization, study habits, comprehension, and retention

Internet Chat Groups

- ADDvisor Chat Group
  www.ADDvisor@yahoogroups.com

Internet Question and Answer Formats

- *ADDitude Magazine*
  www.attitudemag.com

Magazines

- *ADDitude Magazine*
  1720 Bissonnet
  Houston, TX 77005
  1-800-856-2032
  www.attitudemag.com

- *ADDvance Magazine*
  1001 Spring St., Suite 206
  Silver Springs, MD 20910
  1-888-238-8588
  www.advance.com

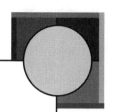

■ *Attention! Magazine*
(a publication of CHADD offered with membership)
8181 Professional Place, Suite 201
Landover, MD 20785
1-800-233-4050
www.chadd.org

Resources for Coaches

■ ADD Coach Academy
17 Googas Road
Slingerlands, NY 12159-9302
1-518-482-3458
www.addca.com

■ American Coaching Association
P.O. Box 353
Lafayette Hill, PA 19144
1-610-825-8572
www.americoach.org

■ OFI-Optimal Functioning Institute
1-865-524-9549
www.addcoach.com

■ Sopris West
4093 Specialty Place
Longmont, CO 80504
1-303-651-2829
www.sopriswest.com
(*The Parent Coach*)

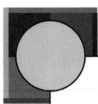

Resources

Resources for Females

■ **Books**

First Star I See (a girl's story about AD/HD-I) - Available through A.D.D. Warehouse

The Phoebe Adventure Series (fun stories about an AD/HD child) - Available through A.D.D. Warehouse

Understanding Girls with AD/HD by Kathleen G. Nadeau, Ph.D., Ellen B. Littman, Ph.D., and Patricia O. Quinn, M.D.

Understanding Women with AD/HD by Kathleen G. Nadeau, Ph.D. and Patricia O. Quinn, M.D.

Women with Attention Deficit Disorder: Embracing Disorganization at Home and in the Workplace by Sari Solden

You Mean I'm not Lazy, Stupid, or Crazy? A Self-Help Book for Adults with Attention Deficit Disorder by Kate Kelly and Peggy Romundo

■ **Periodicals**

ADDitude Magazine (with question and answer line)
www.additudemag.com

ADDvance Magazine
www.addvance.com

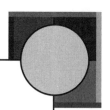

■ **Web Sites:**

www.ADDconsults.com (online consultations)

www.add.org (National Attention Deficit Disorders Association)

www.chadd.org (Children and Adults with Attention-Deficit/Hyperactivity Disorder)

www.addwomen@onelist.com (contact Annie *<12345@aol.com>*)

Support Groups

■ CHADD
8181 Professional Place
Landover, MD 20785
1-800-233-4050
www.chadd.org

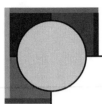

Tests & Checklists Cited

- **ADD-H Comprehensive Teachers and Parent Rating Scale (ACTeRS)**
  Metritech, Inc.
  4106 Fieldstone Rd.
  Champaign, IL 61822
  1-217-398-4868
  www.metritech.com

- **Achenbach Child Behavior Checklist**
  Room 6436
  1 South Prospect Street
  Burlington, VT 05401-3456
  1-802-656-2608
  www.aseba.org

- **The ANSER System**
  Aggregate Neurobehavioral Student Health and Educational Review
  Mel Levine, M.D. (1980, 1985, 1990, 1995)
  Educators Publishing Service, Inc.
  31 Smith Place
  Cambridge, MA 02138-1089
  1-800-435-7728
  www.epsbooks.com

- **BASC, Behavior Assessment System for Children**
  American Guidance Service, Inc.
  4201 Woodland Road
  Circle Pines, MN 55014-1796
  1-800-328-2560
  www.agsnet.com

- **VMI- The Beery-Buktenica Developmental Test of Visual Motor Integration**
  Modern Curriculum Press
  Pearson Learning
  135 South Mount Zion Road
  P.O. Box 2500
  Lebanon, IN 46052
  1-800-526-9907
  www.pearsonlearning.com

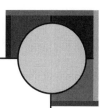

■ **Brown Test of ADD (ADD Scales)**
The Psychological Corp.
555 Academic Court
San Antonio, TX 68204-2498
1-800-211-8378
www.psychcorp.com

■ **Conners' Rating Scales—Revised**
MHS, Inc.
P.O. Box 950
North Tonawanda, NY 14120-0950
1-800-456-3003
www.mhs.com

■ **The Listening Test**
LinguiSystems, Inc.
3100 4th Avenue.
East Moline, IL 61244-9700
1-800-776-4332
www.linguisystems.com

■ **Wechsler Individual Achievement Test**
■ **Wechsler Intelligence Scale for Children—Third Edition**
The Psychological Corporation
19500 Bulverde
San Antonio, TX 78259
1-800-872-1726
www.psychcorp.com

■ **The Woodcock-Johnson III (WJ III) Tests of Cognitive Abilities**
■ **The Woodcock-Johnson III (WJ III) Tests of Achievement**
Riverside Publishing Company
425 Spring Lake Drive
Itasca, IL 60143-2079
1-800-323-9540
www.riverpub.com

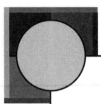

- **AlphaSmart, Inc.**
  973 University Ave.
  Los Gatos, CA 95032
  1-888-274-0680
  www.alphasmart.com
  (handheld keyboard that can be linked to computer printer or main terminal)

- **A.D.D. Warehouse**
  300 N.W. 70th Ave., Ste.102
  Plantation, FL 33317
  1-800-233-9273
  www.addwarehouse.com
  (books)

- **Braille Institute Library Services**
  4555 Executive Drive
  San Diego, CA 92121-3021
  1-800-272-4553
  www.braillelibrary.org
  (books on tape for the blind and learning disabled)

- **Cambridge Development Lab (CDL)**
  86 West St.
  Waltham, MA 02451-1110
  1-800-637-0047
  www.edumatch.com
  (computer software programs)

- **Center for Alternative Learning**
  Learning Disabilities Resources
  P.O. Box 716
  Bryn Mawr, PA 19010
  1-800-869-8336
  (commercially-made semantic webs and maps/carbonless notebook paper)

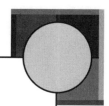

■ **Clearinghouse for Specialized Media and Technology**
P.O. Box 944272
Sacramento, CA 94244-2720
1-916-319-0791
www.cde.ca.gov
(books on tape for the blind and learning disabled)

■ **Crystal Springs Books**
P.O. Box 500
75 Jaffrey Rd.
Peterborough, NH 03458
1-800-321-0401
www.crystalsprings.com.
(colored highlighting tape)

■ **Day-Timers, Inc.**
One Willow Lane
East Texas, PA 18046
1-800-805-2615
www.daytimer.com
(student planners)

■ **Electronic Stores**
(handheld spellers, handheld tape recorders, minute minders, and calendars)

■ **Inspiration Software, Inc.**
7412 SW Beaverton-Hillsdale Hwy.
Suite 102
Portland, OR 97225
1-800-877-4292
www.inspiration.com
(computer software to develop maps and webbing techniques for writing)

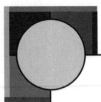

■ **Kurzweil Educational Systems, Inc.**
14 Crosby Dr.
Bedford, MA 01730-1402
1-800-894-5374
www.kurzweiledu.com
(Kurzweil 3000 System - a computer/scanner that reads books orally, highlights words, and provides definitions)

■ **Office Supply Stores**
(Post-it notes, Post-it tabs, colored index cards, colored dots and stars)

■ **PRO-ED**
8700 Shoal Creek Blvd.
Austin, TX 78757-6897
1-800-897-3202
www.proedinc.com
(raised line paper)

■ **Recording for the Blind and Dyslexic**
20 Roszel Road
Princeton, NJ 08540
1-609-452 0606
www.rfbd.org
(books on tape for the blind and learning disabled)

■ **Startwrite**
Idea Maker, Inc.
80 South Redwood Rd., Suite 215
North Salt Lake, UT 84054
1-801-936-7779
www.startwrite.com
(software to create customized handwriting worksheets and lessons)

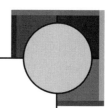

■ **Sunburst Technology**
1900 South Batavia Ave.
Geneva, IL 60134-3399
1-800-321-7511
www.sunburst.com
(computer software to develop keyboard strategies and keyboard pattern
memory; to take ideas from brainstorming to text outline)

■ **WatchMinder**
5405 Alton Parkway #5A
Irvine, CA 92604-3718
1-800-961-0023
www.watchminder.com
(digital watch with beeper and voice messaging to help with personal
organization)

■ **Wizcom Technologies, Ltd.**
257 Gread Rd.
Acton, MA 01720
1-888-777-0552
www.wizcomtech.com
(the Reading Pen)